CONTRACT KILLERS

Geoff Tibballs

B⧫XTREE

First published in Great Britain in 1993 by Boxtree
Limited, Broadwall House, 21 Broadwall,
London SE1 9PL

Copyright © 1993 Geoff Tibballs

10 9 8 7 6 5 4 3 2 1

ISBN: 1 85283 566 4

Phototypeset by Intype, London
Printed and bound in Great Britain by Cox & Wyman,
Reading

A CIP catalogue entry for this book is available from
the British Library

Cover photograph © Jon Tarrant

Acknowlegements

The author would like to thank the following for their help in the preparation of this book: Brighton Central Library, *Bristol Evening Post*, The British Newspaper Library, *East Anglian Daily Times*, *Eastern Daily Press*, *Oxford Mail*, *Peterborough Evening Telegraph*. Thanks also to Boxtree editor Krystyna Zukowska for her alarming interest in the subject matter.

Photographs supplied by The Hulton Deutsch Collection, *Bristol Evening Post*, *Cambridge Evening News*.

CONTENTS

1

A Spinster Spurned

On the face of it, prim, heavily bespectacled, middle-aged spinster Kathleen Calhaem appeared the least likely person imaginable to require the services of a hit man. She looked more like an overbearing maiden aunt than a woman capable of evil machinations. Similarly, Shirley and Hugh Rendell, cricket-loving, churchgoing pillars of the community, seemed to have a perfect marriage. But looks can be very deceiving.

The Rendells lived in a smart bungalow in the village of Yatton, which to millions of holiday-makers each year is little more than a blur as the Inter-City trains that slice through the heart of the district speed out of Bristol on their way down to Devon and Cornwall. It is situated between Bristol and the bustling seaside resort of Weston-super-Mare, which lies some seven miles to the south-west. At forty-six, Shirley Rendell had lived in Yatton all her life and her parents still owned a house nearby. An outgoing, bubbly brunette, she was a popular local figure whom everyone knew as cheerful, kind and friendly. The perfect hostess, she was the life and soul of many a party, a good mingler who was adept at breaking down any signs of awkwardness or pomposity among her guests.

1

Contract Killers

Hugh Rendell, who was four years older, was altogether more reserved. A senior partner in the firm of John Hodge and Co., solicitors based in Weston-super-Mare, he had first met his future wife when she went to work as a telephonist at his office. He was deeply religious and sang as a chorister at Bristol's historic St Mary Redcliffe Church, where he also sometimes played the organ. Shirley Rendell was a regular churchgoer too, but preferred to worship in her home village. They had no children.

Apart from the church, the couple's other principal interest was cricket; to be more precise the fortunes of Somerset County Cricket Club. Hugh Rendell had followed Somerset since his schooldays and had once been treasurer of the club. The late 1970s and early 1980s were exciting times for Somerset cricket as a host of Test stars, such as England all-rounder Ian Botham and West Indian master batsman Viv Richards, guided them to repeated successes in the one-day competitions. Huge crowds flocked to their home matches at the County Ground in Taunton. The Rendells, who became friendly with many of the players, tried never to miss a weekend match at Taunton, where they usually sat in the same seats in the old stand at the river end. They sometimes travelled to away matches, too, and Mrs Rendell, with her eternal picnic basket, was often described as Somerset's number one supporter.

A third person often joined the Rendells at Taunton – sixty-three-year-old, white-haired solicitor Kenneth Pigot, a former vice-president of the club. A father of three grown-up children, Pigot was separated from his wife Lilian and had been friendly with Shirley and Hugh Rendell for some

2

twelve years. He was particularly close to Mrs Rendell, but the relationship did not appear to concern her husband unduly. Her friendship with Pigot was well known, and since it seemed to be so open and platonic, there was little cause for suspicion. Not for a moment did it occur to Hugh Rendell that there might be anything sexual in the relationship – they were simply two people who liked each other's company. After all, if he could not trust a close friend, and a fellow solicitor to boot, such as Kenneth Pigot, who could he trust?

But Shirley Rendell and Pigot were living a lie. Beneath the jolly cricketing banter, they had been enjoying a clandestine affair for some ten years, right under the nose of her gentle, unsuspecting husband. Shortly after the start of the relationship, Pigot had left his family home in Cheddar and moved into lodgings at the Ashcott Inn, Ashcott (a small village just west of Glastonbury), in order to continue the affair. However, he turned down a divorce when it was offered by his wife. What he did not turn down was the opportunity to meet Mrs Rendell whenever humanly possible. He would telephone her three times a day and arrange secret afternoon meetings either in the depths of the Somerset countryside or in anonymous town centre car-parks. Shirley Rendell, ever the good hostess, would arrive with a flask of coffee and home-made sandwiches. It was just like being at cricket – except that there was no husband sitting next to them. And it was not only while Hugh Rendell was at work that they pursued their passion: they also met on Sundays when he was at church.

But, as Shirley Rendell was to discover to her

cost, Kenneth Pigot had another fervent admirer, Kathleen Calhaem. And Miss Calhaem's admiration was a deadly obsession.

It was in 1956 that Kathleen Calhaem moved to the picturesque tourist trap of Cheddar, noted for its cheese and nearby gorge. Born in London and educated at private girls' schools, she had served with distinction in the ATS towards the end of the Second World War. On arriving in Cheddar, she quickly established a reputation for wanting her own way – and usually getting it. Somewhat aloof in manner, she started out as a travelling saleswoman for a cheese straws firm and kept the van in immaculate condition as she toured pubs, shops and wholesalers throughout the West Country. Her sales figures were impressive, too, but her ruthless, single-mindedness revealed itself when she kicked up a fuss about the footballers whom the firm allowed to use the van at weekends. It was invariably returned to her spattered with mud and she complained bitterly to the management. She told one fellow worker that unless those 'dirty, hairy men' stopped defiling it, she would walk out and start up a rival company. Eventually she did quit and, using her undoubted talents as a shrewd, tough businesswoman, allied to a capacity for hard work, she built up a sizeable property and commercial empire in Cheddar Gorge. A fellow trader said of her: 'She slaved from 4.30 in the morning to 10 o'clock at night, every day of the week through the season. I have never known anyone who worked so hard.'

First she bought a small gift shop next to what had once been a motor museum, and then as business boomed in the prosperous 1960s, she expanded to buy other properties including a filling station, a car-park, a small shopping complex and a fish and chip shop. The considerable income accrued from these ventures enabled her to spend her winters cruising and visiting exotic parts of the world. A favourite destination was Morocco, from where she brought back brass and copperware to add to the valuable collection of antiques which adorned the walls of her neat, two-bedroomed bungalow. As a result of her numerous business interests, she was a familiar face in the village but few knew her well. There were occasional mutterings that she was a lesbian and there was even talk of black magic, but these rumours remained unsubstantiated. Kathleen Calhaem liked to keep herself to herself.

One of her forward-thinking innovations was to introduce electronic amusement machines and one-armed bandits. Indeed, she was the first trader in Cheddar to do so. Naturally, she needed a solicitor to handle the licensing – and that was how she first met Kenneth Pigot, senior partner in the country practice of Burrough, Horner and Pigot, based in the village of Wedmore, about five miles south of Cheddar.

At first, the relationship between the wealthy spinster and the solicitor was purely professional, but around 1973 Calhaem became totally infatuated with him. When Pigot later moved to rooms in the Old Post Office at Burtle, near Bridgwater, Calhaem would get up at 4.30 am to intercept him on his way to work. Two or three times a week, she drove to a lay-by in Westhay. From there she would either walk or, taking a folding bicycle from the car, sometimes ride, the few miles along the quiet country lane to Burtle, where she would leave the bicycle in a ditch. Then she waited in the middle of the road. For she knew that Pigot, in military manner, rose at 6.30 each morning without fail and would eventually drive along in his car. He would then stop, give her a lift back to her own vehicle and continue his journey to his office.

This bizarre ritual was performed in the region of five hundred times over a period of more than four years. Much of the time they just talked, but Calhaem prized the few precious moments in the company of the man she loved. Occasionally her persistence was rewarded with something more. There were a few stolen kisses, once he had fondled her breasts and once there had been heavy petting. But full sexual intercourse never took place.

Calhaem knew Pigot's movements down to the last detail. Following a cricket match at Taunton, he discovered her waiting for him on a lonely road. His urges aroused by alcohol, he found himself responding in a more forthright manner than usual. Later, in a statement to the police, she described the encounter thus: 'We stood in the road kissing passionately for about half an hour. It was really wonderful. Then he just left me and walked away. I hoped it would be more. It was such a disappointment.'

To a certain extent, Pigot was flattered by the attention but he steadily began to realise that what to him was a harmless dalliance was beginning to get out of hand. She wrote him love letters but he tore them up. He told her bluntly that he wasn't interested in having a relationship with her. She seemed to accept the situation, but still came back for more. Occasionally, at the end of his tether, he pleaded with his pursuer: 'Get out of my life, leave me alone, stop chasing me.'

But Kathleen Calhaem was not a woman to give up on what she wanted without a fight. What was more, she knew precisely why he was spurning her advances – because he was having an affair with Shirley Rendell. In Calhaem's mind, Mrs Rendell was the sole obstacle blocking her own path to true happiness. With her out of the way, she could have Kenneth Pigot all to herself.

By now Calhaem was bitterly jealous. Shirley Rendell's affair with Pigot occupied her every thought. She hired a private investigator to follow Pigot and frequently undertook some observation work of her own. While the Rendells and Pigot formed a jolly threesome at the County Ground, Taunton, little did they realise that for two summers their movements were being closely scrutinised by a fourth person. Sitting on the opposite side of the ground and menacingly monitoring their behaviour through her powerful binoculars was Kathleen Calhaem. It was self-inflicted pain, but she could not stop herself.

In October 1982, after a total of six years' watching from the shadows, Calhaem decided to take more drastic measures. She hired the services of a new private detective, twenty-nine-year-old Pole, Julian Zajac, who advertised in local newsagents' windows and in the Yellow Pages under the name of Eagle Investigations. To Calhaem, Zajac seemed the answer to her problems. The advertisement made him sound like a latter-day Philip Marlowe, boasting as it did of international coverage, observation and undercover work and a 24-hour service. In truth, Zajac was the sole employee of

Eagle Investigations. He ran the part-time business from his terraced house in Napier Road, Avonmouth, where he lived with his wife Lorraine and their four daughters, aged between one and six. By day, he had the less glamorous job of relief process operator in the furnace at Commonwealth Smelting in Avonmouth.

Zajac had started up the agency in 1977, using the name Julian Jones. His strange double life remained a secret from his work-mates but then again, none of them really knew him anyway. He was a loner, described as an 'edgy' man who became part of their conversation only when they teased him about his nationality, of which he was fiercely proud. He had just one friend at Commonwealth Smelting, Roy Daniels.

Zajac's investigative work was usually routine enough, the same old round of insurance claims and divorce cases. But, like all small-time private eyes, he dreamed of 'the big one', the case the Yard was unable to crack. When the phone rang that October, he had no reason to think that this case would be anything out of the ordinary. The client was someone who asked whether he was available for surveillance work. No name was left, just details of a meeting-place. The voice was deep and masculine, and so when he went to the arranged rendezvous at the Hope and Anchor public house in the west Bristol suburb of Shirehampton, he was expecting to do business with a man. Instead he found the gravel-voiced Kathleen Calhaem. Overcoming his initial surprise, he listened as she outlined the assignment. She said she wanted him to follow someone in the Cheddar area, a friend whom she was worried was being harassed. She went on to tell Zajac that the person she wanted followed, on Mondays, Wednesdays and Fridays, was a Mr Pigot, who was a solicitor in the village of Wedmore. Zajac was paid a £50 retainer.

Tackling the task with his customary expertise, Zajac went about his observation. He followed Pigot to a shopping centre car-park and inevitably saw the solicitor meet Mrs Rendell.

Eager to report his progress, Zajac arranged another meeting with Calhaem at the Hope and Anchor. The two developed a code by which he would recognise her (she had still not identified herself) when she called. She was to say '12 o'clock.' When Zajac imparted the news of his discovery at their appointed destination, Calhaem indicated that she wished some harm to come to a woman. She mentioned 'getting rid of' someone. Zajac was later to claim that he did not take her seriously. 'I just felt she had more money than sense and that in time she would realise how stupid she had been.' But at their next meeting, events took a more sinister turn.

This third liaison occurred in the car-park of the Progress Inn at Shirehampton. Calhaem said she wanted a woman killed. When asked who, she told Zajac that he had already seen her – Shirley Rendell.

'How much are you prepared to pay?' asked Zajac.

'£5,000,' replied Calhaem.

'It will probably cost twice as much,' said Zajac.

Calhaem agreed to his demands but told him that in a couple of months she could only lay her hands on £5,000 in cash. She said she could, however, pay the remainder about a year later or give

9

him a valuable gold or silver bracelet in lieu of the second instalment. Before departing, Calhaem provided him with details of the movements of the Rendells, plus the address of their bungalow in Henley Lane, Yatton.

It had been agreed that the first £5,000 would be paid in a meeting at Calhaem's home and that she would call when she had got the money. Even a retired businesswoman of her means needed time to put together that amount of cash.

Zajac waited patiently until, on 28 January 1983, the phone rang. It was '12 o'clock' – Calhaem telling him to come and pick up the money from her home in The Link, Cheddar.

He arrived to find a cul-de-sac resplendent with highly desirable dwellings. But at Calhaem's bungalow, the atmosphere was distinctly eerie, like something out of a Hitchcock movie. As his would-be employer ushered him in, he became aware that the entire house was shrouded in darkness, except for the flickering light from the television set. Calhaem told him to put on a pair of ladies' gloves because she did not want his fingerprints in the house, and poured him a brandy to calm his nerves. She too was wearing gloves. He inquired about the money and she pointed to a package on the sideboard, adding that there was no need to worry about the contents because it was all there. Paying attention to detail like a seasoned professional, she had spent most of the previous evening wiping each note carefully with surgical spirit so that there would be no trace of her fingerprints on them. Then she asked Zajac how he intended to carry out the killing. He hesitated and Calhaem suggested that if Mrs Rendell was found to have been sexually assaulted before she was killed, the police would believe that was the motive. 'And,' she added venomously, 'it would go very well with the type of life she led.'

Kathleen Calhaem's wicked plan came to fruition a month later, on 23 February. The previous week, on 14 February, Zajac had bought two shotguns and on the morning of the 23rd he stole a white Mini from a car-park at Commonwealth Smelting, drove to Yatton and parked near the Rendells' bungalow. Shirley Rendell was alone in the house, husband Hugh having left for a bogus 9.30 am appointment arranged by Zajac under a false name to ensure that he was out of the way. To build up his courage, Zajac sat in the car and finished off the remainder of a bottle of vodka. It seemed to have the required effect and after a few minutes, he pulled up outside the bungalow and walked up the drive carrying a hammer, a knife and a parcel.

It was 9.00 am, and Mrs Rendell was in her bedroom on the phone to a local builder when she saw the old car stop outside her house and a man get out with a gift-wrapped parcel in his left hand. As he came up the drive, she interrupted her call, eager to discover the contents of the parcel. She might not have been so keen had she known that the gift wrapping concealed a box, and that in the box was a shotgun. It was a peaceful neighbourhood, so she half-opened the front door to let the mystery man with the parcel know that there was someone at home. After all, the last thing she wanted was for him to go away again. She then dashed back to the phone to tell the builder that she would be in touch later and returned to the front door.

'Can you sign for this parcel, please?' said the caller.

Shirley Rendell went back indoors to fetch a pen. Zajac placed the parcel on the floor just inside the front door, entered the hallway and grabbed her from behind. She struggled and screamed whereupon he produced the hammer from his coat pocket and attacked her repeatedly, raining sufficient blows on her head and with such ferocity to cause multiple fractures of the skull. He then took a knife, also from his coat pocket, and stabbed her ten times in the throat. The deed done, he drove off and later destroyed a black plastic bin liner, containing bloodstained clothing, in a vat of molten metal at the factory where he worked.

Shirley Rendell's body lay there for nine hours until 6.00 pm, when husband Hugh arrived home from work as usual. One of the things he was waiting to tell her about was the strange early-morning appointment that never was. Instead his thoughts were immediately diverted when he opened the front door and stepped into the hallway to find it smeared with blood. He glanced down and saw the body of his wife. Her hands were slashed from her attempts to defend herself against Zajac's onslaught.

Police with tracker dogs searched the grounds of the adjoining cricket club in an attempt to find the murder weapon. They believed they were looking for something like a hammer or a heavy spanner. Mrs Rendell had not been sexually assaulted and nothing seemed to be missing from the house. Nor had the house been forcibly entered, leading the police to conclude that she had opened her door to the killer. There was therefore a distinct possibility that she may have known her assailant.

Of course, the most baffling aspect of the case at that stage was the motive. There was none. A respectable, happily married woman, apparently without an enemy in the world, had been bludgeoned to death in her own home in the furtherance neither of sexual gratification nor robbery. Neighbours spoke warmly of the loss of a dear friend. Two days after the murder, Hugh Rendell, still ignorant of his wife's duplicity, said: 'I cannot think of any reason why anyone should attack her. I feel sorry for them, because they do not realise what they have done.'

The inquest at Weston-super-Mare revealed that Shirley Rendell had died from a brain haemorrhage caused by multiple fractures of the skull. The police reopened files into the killing of Mrs Beryl Culverwell, a stockbroker's wife who had been battered to death in Bath in 1978, because there were 'certain similarities' between the two murders. But that particular trail led nowhere.

Kathleen Calhaem's devilish design seemed to have worked perfectly, but she had reckoned without one thing: the frailty of human nature. Above all, the frailty of the man she had hired to carry out her dirty work, Julian Zajac. For while Calhaem remained cold and brutally calculating, Zajac lived in a different world altogether, a fantasy world in which he combined the drudgery of work in the furnace with the excitement of being a private eye. He was tired of being treated as a joke by his workmates and could not wait to boast about what he had done. Maybe then they would think he was somebody. So he told his sole confidant at Commonwealth Smelting, Roy Daniels, that there had been a plot to kill Shirley Rendell, and that he had carried it out. At first, the disbelieving Daniels failed to take him seriously, but when he realised that this was not one of Zajac's daydreams, he informed the police.

Zajac was arrested, but still there was nothing positive to link him with Calhaem. When investigations into Shirley Rendell's background revealed the Calhaem connection, the businesswoman was questioned but brazenly told police that she was being blackmailed and was released after a couple of days. The police still thought they had enough to charge both Zajac and Calhaem with murder, but it appeared that she had been too clever for the law because on 27 June she was freed after the Director of Public Prosecutions ruled that there was insufficient evidence to proceed against her.

So Zajac was left to face the consequences alone. But although he was to claim subsequently that he lived in fear of Calhaem, he eventually decided that it was time to tell the whole story – and to name names. At his trial at Birmingham Crown Court in September 1983, he pleaded guilty to the murder of Shirley Rendell and made a new statement implicating the fifty-seven-year-old Cheddar spinster. Mr Roger Titheridge QC, for the prosecution, said that the murder was 'counselled and procured' by a woman still at liberty. That situation was swiftly rectified. The day after her hired hit man was sentenced to life imprisonment, Calhaem was rearrested at her bungalow.

Calhaem's trial was fixed for the following January at Winchester Crown Court. The star prosecution witness was Julian Zajac. When the charge

14

of murdering Mrs Rendell was put to her on the first day, Calhaem replied: 'Not guilty, my lord.' They were to be the only words she spoke throughout the entire trial.

But Zajac had plenty to say. In a statement to the police he said of Calhaem: 'I feel she is such an evil person, for without her I would never have got involved. She is such a strong personality; she made me so vulnerable; she made me feel like a small boy with her.' And he told the jury: 'Privately, I feared Miss Calhaem more than the law.'

Defence counsel Mr George Carman QC suggested that by calling Calhaem an evil person, Zajac was trying to put the blame for his own crime mainly on her shoulders. Zajac said that was incorrect and added: 'I described her as an evil person because I felt a psychological pressure on me to carry out her instructions. If anyone asked someone else to kill someone, they are obviously as evil as I ended up being.'

Of the murder itself, Zajac said that he had not wanted to go through with the killing but had been driven on by Calhaem's forceful personality and by the fact that he had already spent some of the contract money. He claimed that from the time he took the money to the time he walked up to the bungalow in Henley Lane, Yatton he never intended to fulfil the mission to kill. He planned to deceive Calhaem by acting out a charade, trying to pretend he had bungled the murder. On entering the house and confronting Mrs Rendell, he said: 'I grabbed at her and she started screaming and struggling. We fell to the floor. I tried to calm her down and said: "Do not worry, I have only come here to rob you.' And I hit her. I had the hammer and the knife in my coat pocket because I had taken them there so she would think someone had been there to kill her. I lost my head. I cannot remember how many times I hit her with the hammer. I stood up thinking, what have I done?' She was still alive so I panicked and stabbed her in the throat with the knife and then ran out.'

Prosecuting counsel said of Zajac: 'He did not know Mrs Rendell. He had no reason of his own, no personal motive to harm her or to kill her. He did it because he was put up to it by the defendant now in the dock. She did it, in a nutshell, for two reasons: love for another man, called Kenneth Pigot, and jealousy of Shirley Rendell.'

When Pigot took the stand, Mr Carman asked him: 'With your experience of life and the world, would you realise the awful danger of toying in any way with the affections of a middle-aged spinster lady?'

'No,' replied Pigot, 'I am afraid I would not. I think as far as women are concerned I am rather naïve.' As Pigot spoke those last few words, Calhaem, who throughout the trial had watched every witness intently with the notable exception of the man she loved, felt compelled to dart a quick glance in his direction. Then she returned her gaze to the piece of paper on which she was copiously taking notes.

Pigot also testified that Calhaem had once written to him offering to give him part of her estate so that he could set up home with Mrs Rendell. Even in a case as strange as this, it was indeed a curious suggestion.

Kathleen Calhaem herself did not give evidence, and the only defence witness was an anonymous convicted double murderer. This individual, who was referred to only as 'Mr X' but who was believed to be a notorious gangland boss, spoke of conversations he claimed to have had with Zajac while the latter was awaiting trial at Horfield Prison near Bristol. He told the court that Zajac was prepared to give false evidence implicating Calhaem in order to obtain a lighter sentence for himself.

But the jury were unimpressed by his story and at the end of the eighteen-day trial, they required just four hours' deliberation before returning a unanimous verdict of guilty against Kathleen Calhaem for the murder of Shirley Rendell. On 31 January 1984, Calhaem was jailed for life. Dressed immaculately as ever, her grey-tinted hair complemented by a tweed skirt, white jumper and paisley scarf, and with her true feelings hidden behind those forbidding black horn-rimmed spectacles, she showed no hint of emotion as she was sentenced. She stood stiffly to attention as Mr Justice Stuart-Smith told her: 'Your actions, which led to the death of Mrs Rendell, were those of a cold, calculating and evil woman.' She gave a slight bow from the waist as she was led away to the cells.

Afterwards Mr George Carman called it a trial 'so bizarre and macabre it makes Dallas sound like a children's bedtime story'.

At The Link in Cheddar, the exclusive cul-de-sac where Calhaem hatched her murder plan, neighbours were still coming to terms with the extraordinary sequence of events. One man said: 'I think everybody thought she was guilty, but they somehow believed she would get off.'

And so this quiet corner of England was left to pick up the pieces and return to the normality it had enjoyed before being harshly plunged into the national spotlight. The toll had been high. Not only was Shirley Rendell dead, but three weeks after the murder her father had also collapsed and died. Friends said it had been the shock that had killed him. The honest, God-fearing Hugh Rendell had broken down in court as details of his wife's secret love-life became public knowledge. Only his faith carried him through the ordeal. And shortly before the trial, Kenneth Pigot collapsed in his office in Wedmore, suffering from what was said at the time to be 'severe exhaustion'. When he gave evidence, he had to do so with a nurse in attendance. A father of four young girls was in prison and a once respectable lady, who could have lived a comfortable, even luxurious retirement, the reward for a life of hard work, was now also behind bars. And all in the name of love.

But this was no ordinary love. This was a fatal attraction. And even when confronted with the enormity of her sins, Kathleen Calhaem's obsession remained for all to see. While in her cell awaiting trial, she clung to a tiny, almost insignificant, memento of Pigot: the butt of a cigar he had smoked during a visit. When a detective casually threw it into the corridor, she pleaded for it to be given back, saying: 'I have been keeping it there as it reminds me of Kenneth.' There were tears in her eyes.

2

Here Comes the Judge

It was a warm evening in early June 1955. The exclusive Florida resort of Manalapan, eleven miles south of Palm Beach, gently reverberated to the sounds of the Atlantic waves lapping on to the shore. On the streets all was quiet, apart from a large car slowly circling an isolated beach house. For the next three hours the mystery vehicle continued to cruise around the neighbourhood. Inside were three men, Judge Joseph Peel, who was armed with a pistol, and his two hired hit men, Floyd Holzapfel and Bobby Lincoln. The object of their interest was the occupant of the house, Judge Curtis Chillingworth, a long-serving and respected guardian of the law in Florida. Fortunately for him, his would-be assassins, seeing no car in the drive, came to the conclusion that he was not at home that evening and abandoned their pursuit around midnight. But it was merely a stay of execution.

Joseph Alexander Peel and Curtis Eugene Chillingworth were both judges in the town of West Palm Beach, the poor neighbour to the millionaires' playground. They were known as 'The Little Judge' and 'The Big Judge' respectively. However, their chosen profession was just about the only thing they had in common.

Judge Chillingworth was an imposing figure, capable of putting the fear of God into defendants and lawyers alike. By 1955, he had sat on the bench for thirty-two years and had acquired the reputation of being a somewhat puritanical individual, particularly when dealing with unfaithful men in divorce cases. At fifty-eight, the judge himself had been happily married to his wife Marjorie for thirty-five years and had no time for philanderers.

Judge Peel was thirty-one and flash, a political glamour-boy who dreamed of being governor. With a silver tongue and a winning smile, he revelled in the trappings of success. He had an image to maintain and drove an air-conditioned white Cadillac, wore white linen suits and had been known to change shirts four or five times a day. But he funded his extravagant lifestyle by running rackets.

In 1953, Judge Peel, who was also permitted to practise as an attorney, was approached by twenty-nine-year-old Floyd Holzapfel on a legal matter. Holzapfel was newly arrived in West Palm Beach, and had had what could best be described as a chequered career. His parents had split up when he was young, and at sixteen he went to stay with his father, Cleo, in Los Angeles. He hero-worshipped his father and saw him as a prominent member of the LA underworld, once boasting: 'I've buried three fellows for my father.' In truth, Cleo Holzapfel had never been involved in anything more serious than petty crime, including two arrests on suspicion of bookmaking and one for drunken driving. But Floyd liked to impress. After the war, by now married to the first of his four wives, he moved to Oklahoma City. He persuaded the police department there that he had been a wartime investigator and, impressed by recommendations from former teachers and his well-connected mother-in-law, they took him on as a fingerprint clerk. He was kicked out after just three months when rumours that he was spending most of his duty hours offering protection to local prostitutes reached the ears of his superiors.

Holzapfel, who had somewhat incongruously acquired the nickname Lucky, went into a steady decline. In August 1946, he visited his father in California and was promptly sentenced to sixty days in jail for bookmaking. Returning once more to Oklahoma City, he and two friends carried out a succession of small-time armed robberies, none of which netted more than $100. True to character, he later bragged to anyone who would listen that the trio had robbed an armoured truck of $150,000. Holzapfel paid for his crimes with seventeen months in prison.

Then, in another remarkable career change, again backed by any number of upright citizens who seemed eager to set him on the path to righteousness, Holzapfel began to study to become a lawyer. But when a policeman recognised him and told his new college friends about his murky past, Holzapfel was finished. He headed for Miami Beach, where he married his third wife and embarked on a number of get-rich-quick schemes. But none of the schemes got him rich quick enough. Increasingly restless, in 1952 he moved the family sixty miles north to West Palm Beach. He quickly landed a job cleaning cars and, in the course of his work, needed some form of legal help. His boss recommended the much-loved Judge Peel, who had earned the reputation for being able to fix just about anything.

The judge was indeed able to help, and the two men soon became firm friends, to the point of being almost inseparable. In 1954, Holzapfel was a fervent campaigner on Peel's re-election trail and effectively became his second-in-command, responsible for the smooth day-to-day running of his shady business empire. Among their operations was selling protection to moonshiners and operators of Bolita, a Florida version of the numbers racket. In a good week, they raked in as much as $3,000.

After years of toiling in dead-end jobs, Holzapfel loved the attention generated by his new-found employer. He drove around town in Peel's second car, a Lincoln, and wore a gun strapped to his leg, and when performing errands, would proudly announce: 'The judge sent me.'

As their illicit enterprises continued to flourish, Peel told Holzapfel of his ambitions to become governor. And his willing henchman was left in no doubt that any glory would be reflected on himself. The guy who had fantasised about having a hoodlum father and of robbing an armoured truck would be elevated to the status of one of the big shots in Florida. But there was one fly in the ointment, one barrier to this life of power and wealth: Judge Chillingworth.

Peel had crossed swords with Chillingworth once before when he had been caught representing both sides in a divorce action. For this highly unethical practice, he had been officially rebuked by Chillingworth. Now he broke the rules again, also with a divorce case, and this time the word around town was that Judge Chillingworth, who had kept quiet about the first misdemeanour, was determined to see the younger man disbarred. A fellow attorney confided to Peel: 'That squinty-eyed old bastard is going to take care of you.'

Peel was reduced to a state of panic. He could envisage his whole empire crumbling around him. As he told Holzapfel, 'It would ruin my career and our business.'

There was only one thing for it. Judge Chillingworth had to be eliminated. Holzapfel later insisted that the suggestion appalled him. 'Joe Peel told me I was his only friend in the world, his best friend. If I killed Chillingworth I would be his friend for life. "That's the only solution" he said. I told him he was crazy.'

Crazy or not, Peel was deadly serious. Over the next month, using his considerable powers of persuasion, he eventually coerced Holzapfel into going along with the murder plot and, having the in-built abhorrence of blood that goes with high office, he certainly was not going to dirty his own hands carrying out the killing. 'Naturally, I couldn't do it personally,' he told Holzapfel. 'It's got to be you.'

'Well, I'll have to have help,' replied Holzapfel. 'How about Bobby Lincoln?'

Bobby Lincoln was another, smaller cog in the Peel-Holzapfel wheel of fortune. A man of few words, he owned taxis and pool-rooms and ran the rackets in the region of West Palm Beach known as 'Coloured Town'. His paymaster was Peel. Lincoln was not a violent man but joined the conspiracy simply because he was scared of The Little Judge. Lincoln was later to testify: 'I have got a wife and a child and I want them to live and I wanted to live, too.'

Peel and Holzapfel embroiled Lincoln in their

scheme one afternoon in June 1955. They drove out to Lincoln's house and took him to a lonely dirt track off Highway 1. There Peel said: 'Bobby, a man is trying to ruin us and I have got to kill him.'

'What's he trying to do?' asked Lincoln.

'Well, he's going to ruin everything that we have worked for and everything that we are doing.'

By now, especially after Peel had promised him a sizeable financial reward for carrying out the murder, Holzapfel seemed to have overcome his initial reservations and was well into his stride. He told Peel that he would need to know thorough details of Judge Chillingworth's routine, and indeed those of his wife Marjorie. Peel said that Chillingworth was a creature of habit. As an added bonus, there were no servants in the house to worry about. However, Peel added chillingly, if anyone else did happen to be in the house at the time, they too would have to be disposed of.

The plotters wasted no time on further preparations, and that was how they came to be touring around the judge's summer beach house in Manalapan that same evening. Following the aborted mission, several more reconnaissance trips were undertaken in the hope of catching at least a sight of Judge Chillingworth. The trio drew a blank until finally Peel spotted him on the street in Manalapan. 'There he is! There he is!' he exclaimed excitedly.

Holzapfel committed Judge Chillingworth's face to memory, and a few evenings later decided he was ready to fulfil his part of the bargain. He approached the secluded house, intending to shoot the judge when he answered the door. But at the last minute, within a few yards of the door, Holzapfel's nerve failed him and he made a hasty exit.

Perhaps the job of killing such a noted public figure was too big for him after all.

As the threat of his disbarment intensified, Peel became increasingly frustrated by the fact that Judge Chillingworth was still in circulation. Neither of his hired hit men seemed particularly adept. At this rate, Chillingworth would outlive them all. So the ever-inventive Peel came up with a new murder plan whereby Chillingworth would be snatched from his house, taken by boat out to sea and drowned. Peel's enthusiasm was matched by Holzapfel's, the clinching factor being that there was little chance of the body ever being recovered and that therefore he and Lincoln were not likely to be ever brought to justice. As it turned out, they were right in the first assumption but not in the second.

To transport them down the coast, Holzapfel bought a small fishing boat for $350 as well as two rolls of adhesive tape, two strong clotheslines, two pairs of gloves, two Army belts and, most importantly, a number of lead sinker weights to put into the pockets of the belts.

Just before 9.00 pm on 14 June 1955, while Peel stayed at home to watch *The $64,000 Question* on television with his wife in order to establish an alibi, Holzapfel collected Lincoln. Not only was the weather fine for the excursion but Peel had assured them that Judge Chillingworth would be alone in the house because his wife was staying with relatives. The two hired hands carried three guns, including a shotgun, a present from Peel to Lincoln for services rendered. There was also a .38 target pistol which Peel had lent Holzapfel. Ironically, it had originally been a gift to Peel from a police lieutenant.

The pair drove to the Blue Heron Dock in nearby Riviera and headed out in the boat towards Manalapan. Even on a tranquil night such as this, it was a long journey in a small craft powered by nothing more than a converted car engine, but eventually they reached their destination, parking some six feet from the shore. Their nerves calmed by a few swigs of whiskey en route, they put their plan into action. Holzapfel told Lincoln: 'You stay with the boat and I will call if I need you.' With that, he climbed the steps which led up to the house.

It was shortly after midnight when Holzapfel, wearing a yachting cap to give the impression that he was a sailor in distress, knocked on the door. Judge Chillingworth was in bed. He had spent the evening with friends but had returned home shortly after 10.00 pm to prepare himself for a strenuous day in court. Wearing a pair of pink pyjamas that had seen better days, he trustingly opened the door.

'Are you Judge Chillingworth?' asked Holzapfel.

'I am,' answered the judge.

At that, Holzapfel produced his pistol and, as a precautionary measure, demanded: 'Is there anyone else in the house?'

To the hit man's horror, the judge called his wife. This was not part of the plan. Realising he would require the services of an extra pair of hands, Holzapfel summoned Lincoln from the beach. While Holzapfel kept his gun trained on Judge and Marjorie Chillingworth, Lincoln checked to make sure there were no other unexpected guests in the house. Confident that the house was now empty, Lincoln, who still did not appear to have grasped the finer points of the exercise, blurted out: 'What are you going to do with these people, Floyd?'

According to Lincoln, Holzapfel replied: 'I am going to take these people and put them on the boat. We are going to have to send them off for a few days. These are the people who are going to mess up Joe.'

Quite why Holzapfel should even risk mentioning the name of their benefactor is beyond comprehension.

Bound with the adhesive tape and with ropes around their necks, the Chillingworths were led down the steps to the beach. But before escorting Marjorie Chillingworth, Holzapfel searched the house for cash. Finding the judge's wallet, he removed two ten-dollar notes but left behind some small change because Peel had instructed him not to make it look like a robbery. Peel did not want there to be any hint of a crime at all – he hoped that the investigating authorities would conclude that the couple had accidentally been swept out to sea while going for a late-night swim.

Up ahead, Judge Chillingworth tried to plead for the safety of himself and his wife. He whispered to Lincoln: 'Boy, you take care of us in this and you will never have to work any more.' But Lincoln was in too deep now to back out – he knew that his only hope of getting out of this mess was for the Chillingworths to disappear off the face of the earth and for everyone to keep their mouths shut.

At one point, Mrs Chillingworth succeeded in working her gag loose but a blow from Holzapfel's pistol silenced her screams. There was another anxious moment for the two hit men when they realised they were missing one of their guns. There was no way they could head out to sea leaving a shred of evidence behind, let alone a gun. They were mightily relieved when Holzapfel found it on the beach.

As they headed out to sea in the boat, Holzapfel strapped the divers' weights around Marjorie Chillingworth's waist. On seeing this, the judge must have sensed his wife's impending fate for he said softly, 'Remember, I love you.'

Mrs Chillingworth answered, 'I love you too.'

The next moment, Holzapfel lifted her up and hurled her into the Atlantic Ocean. She made no sound and was never seen again.

Now it was the judge's turn. Holzapfel fetched the other weights – even though he had only expected to have to send one person to a watery grave, he had taken the precaution of bringing along sufficient weights for two. But the judge was not going to give up without a struggle, and before Holzapfel could put the weights on him, he jumped into the sea. Swimming was virtually impossible because his hands and feet were still tightly bound, but the pair were petrified in case he somehow managed to escape.

Holzapfel, who was steering the boat, screamed: 'Hit him, Bobby, hit him!'

'Hit him with what?'

'Hit him with the shotgun!'

Still the judge continued to thrash about in the water, fighting for his life. Lincoln's blow had hardly any impact and so Holzapfel seized the weapon and, holding it by the barrel, bludgeoned the judge with such force that the stock of the gun broke. They knew that they dare not shoot him for fear of the noise it would make.

The judge's brave struggle was finally cruelly

ended when, in the words of Bobby Lincoln, 'Floyd reached down and he got the rope that the anchor was on. He wrapped it around and around the man's neck. He dropped the anchor over the side of the boat and he cut the rope, and he took his foot and put it against the man's head and shoved him from between my arms out in the water and he went down and never came up no more.'

At home, having watched a policeman win on *The $64,000 Question*, Peel waited anxiously for news. At last the phone rang. It was Holzapfel with the coded message to signify that the mission had been successfully accomplished: 'The motor has been fixed.'

Holzapfel, who was soaked to the skin, demanded a clean shirt. Throwing caution to the wind, Peel drove down to Riviera to meet his heroes.

'How was it?' he asked enthusiastically.

Holzapfel did not share his elation and instead complained about the presence of Mrs Chillingworth. Peel replied: 'Honest to God, I didn't know she'd be there.'

He wanted to know all the gruesome details straight away, but Holzapfel was in no mood for small talk. He insisted: 'Just leave me alone and let me go home.'

The first signs of disquiet about Judge Chillingworth's fate surfaced the following morning when he failed to show up for his court sitting. This was totally out of character, for he could always be relied upon to be in court at 8.00 am sharp. That same day, 15 June, two carpenters called at his house but received no reply. The car was in the garage.

Peel's hopes of convincing the world that the judge and his wife had met with an accident were scuppered by the discovery of bloodstains on the steps leading from the house down to the beach. They were the result of the gun-butt blow with which Holzapfel had silenced Mrs Chillingworth's screams. Furthermore, on the beach itself there were footprints and indications of a scuffle.

Peel nearly blew everything himself just two days after the murder while he was having lunch with Holzapfel at a restaurant in downtown West Palm Beach. A local funeral director stopped by at their table and imparted the news. 'I just got a call that Mr and Mrs Chillingworth were found on the beach by their home.'

Peel leaped to his feet and spluttered: 'It isn't possible!'

The 'news' turned out to be a false alarm, one of many that would ring out across Palm Beach over the next few years. And luckily for Peel, nobody in the restaurant thought anything more of his outburst. Rewards totalling $160,000 were offered but with no trace of the bodies, there appeared little prospect of the case ever being solved. Everyone had their pet theories, of course, but for the want of concrete evidence, such rumours were nothing more than idle speculation. Indeed, they might have remained so today had not Judge Peel made one fatal mistake: he forgot to look after Floyd Holzapfel.

His most serious omission of all was not paying his hired killer. This, plus the murder of Mrs Chillingworth, which continued to prey on his mind, resulted in Holzapfel becoming increasingly disenchanted. He had been led to believe that the removal of Judge Chillingworth would clear the way for the Peel-Holzapfel empire to flourish; that after years of drudgery, he would finally live up to his nickname of Lucky. Instead, not only had he taken all the risks but he had not been properly paid. He had never even got back the money he had forked out for the boat.

What was more, Peel's empire was beginning to fall apart. Chillingworth's role as his chief persecutor had been taken over by local prosecutor Phil O'Connell. If anything, O'Connell was an even bigger danger to Peel's wellbeing than the late judge, because he appeared to know all about Peel's racketeering. The situation reached the stage where Peel and Holzapfel considered making O'Connell their next murder victim, and in fact they did case his home in the south end of West Palm Beach in much the same way as they had driven to Manalapan to seek out Judge Chillingworth. But the plan was dropped, partly because even Peel must have realised that he could not go around eliminating all of his enemies. And sooner or later, someone was bound to put two and two together. Besides, so many stories had spread about his dubious activities that there was now no possibility whatsoever of his ever sitting in the governor's chair. And before long, these stories escalated to the point where Peel was forced to resign as a judge and quit the bar altogether, the very thing he had so desperately sought to avoid by ordering the murder of Judge Chillingworth. The Chillingworths really had died in vain.

Despite his frustration, Holzapfel continued to work for Peel whenever the latter hit upon a money-making scheme. And Holzapfel was constantly in need of cash since his fourth wife was something of a free spender. He was even reduced to borrowing from Bobby Lincoln, whose own concerns were doing very nicely. Allegedly, one of Peel's plans for raising capital was secretly to insure the life of Harold Gray, a legitimate young lawyer who had once worked for him, for $100,000 and then have him murdered by Holzapfel. The 'hit' was to take place in a seedy West Palm Beach nightclub in which Peel had acquired a share. Peel and Gray arrived late one night when the place was closed and Holzapfel, who worked there as a barman, suddenly leaped out of the darkness and began beating Gray fiercely over the head. Eventually Peel, who, as we know, could not bear the sight of blood, called him off. Peel, Holzapfel and a character by the name of James W. Yenzer, who had sold Peel the insurance policy, were charged with plotting Gray's murder. It was later alleged that Holzapfel had intended to drown Gray but that Peel had arrived with the intended victim before the preparations were finished. In the event, the case against the three was dropped due to technicalities. But as justice slowly took its course against Joe Peel, a lot more was to be heard of James Yenzer.

In the meantime, Holzapfel developed an unhealthy interest in Bobby Lincoln's moonshine operation, until it was busted by the FBI and Lincoln and seventy-five others wound up in prison. The bootleggers incorrectly assumed that a young colleague, Lew Gene Harvey, had informed on them. Holzapfel kindly offered to wipe him out for $50,000, although Lincoln later testified that Holzapfel eventually did it for nothing.

Using the alias John Lynch, Holzapfel wormed

his way into Harvey's acquaintance by offering him a slice of the action in a scheme to export stolen cars to South America. On 3 November 1958, Holzapfel collected Harvey from his house, on the pretence of driving him to Miami for a business meeting. They broke their journey to pick up Lincoln. Instead of heading for Miami, Holzapfel drove to a canal near West Palm Beach and, holding him at gunpoint, trussed and handcuffed the helpless Harvey and dragged him on to a boat. He then coldly shot Harvey in the back of the head and dumped him in the canal with the aid of a concrete block tied to his legs. Holzapfel was no longer just an amateur murderer, he had graduated to a professional contract killer.

Although it failed to do Harvey himself much good, he had urged his wife to write down the number of the car driven by 'Lynch' when it came to pick him up. Harvey, too, had heard the rumours that he was supposed to have grassed on his fellow bootleggers and he was fearful of reprisals.

When her husband failed to return home, Mrs Harvey reported the car number-plate to the sheriff's office. It was traced to Holzapfel. Then, four days after the murder, despite Holzapfel's elaborate weighing-down exercise, Harvey's body somehow floated to the canal surface and was found by a fisherman. Harvey was identified by his fingerprints.

Led by agents Ross Anderson and Henry J. Lovern, the Florida Sheriffs' Bureau devoted hours of manpower to the investigation, their enthusiasm fuelled by a tip-off from the mysterious James Yenzer, who thought he might have some information on the Chillingworth affair. This was indeed welcome news, for despite an immense amount of publicity, in the three and a half years since the Chillingworths had disappeared the authorities had come no nearer to solving the case.

A common factor began to emerge: Floyd Holzapfel. There was Holzapfel's association with Lincoln and that of Lincoln with Harvey; Holzapfel's role in the Harold Gray case and his links with Peel; the discovery that both Holzapfel and Lincoln had been protected by Peel while running their rackets. And, potentially the most damning of all, the very real possibility that the Chillingworths may have been drowned in a remarkably similar manner to Lew Harvey. The net was beginning to close in on Holzapfel.

It was then that James Yenzer began to play a crucial part in the whole sorry affair. In the wake of the Gray business, he and Holzapfel had been employed as house detectives at an exclusive Miami Beach hotel. At first the pair got along well enough but after a while Yenzer developed an intense dislike of his new partner. Now, for a fee of $125 a week plus expenses, in addition to the expectation of the substantial reward money, Yenzer was prepared to help the Sheriffs' Bureau nail Floyd Holzapfel – and with him possibly an even bigger fish.

Yenzer's first job as an informant involved an arms hijack which Holzapfel had planned. Yenzer offered to help out his old buddy but at the same time alerted the police. In the ensuing shoot-out, Yenzer was allowed to escape but Holzapfel, who still had no idea of Yenzer's double-dealing, was arrested and sentenced to fifteen years. On appeal, he was released on $20,000 bail, the money being put up by a sympathetic ex-cop named Jim Wilber.

One night in March 1959, his tongue loosened by alcohol, Holzapfel cautiously confided to Yenzer that he had been involved in some way in the Chillingworth affair. Liaising with the Sheriffs' Bureau, Yenzer stirred things up by paying a visit to his other old pal, Joe Peel. Yenzer spoke of Holzapfel's revelation that Peel had hired someone to kill Judge Chillingworth.

Peel's reaction was: 'Floyd should be careful of what he says and who he talks to.'

A few months later, Yenzer again played on Peel's vulnerability, suggesting to him that Holzapfel would be a considerable threat to him if he started opening his mouth to a wider audience. Yenzer pointed out that Holzapfel was still aggrieved at not having been paid for his work.

By October, Peel was sufficiently rattled to ask Yenzer to kill Holzapfel. Peel wanted to know how much he would charge and Yenzer quoted a sum of between $5,000 and $10,000, but, for old times' sake, he agreed to do it for $2,000. Peel suggested that Yenzer should drown Holzapfel from a boat so that the body would never be found. Somehow that idea had a familiar ring to it.

In an attempt to keep Holzapfel sweet, Peel invited him to become a partner in an investment business called the Insured Capital Corporation. But beneath the surface charm and bonhomie, Peel saw Holzapfel's real future as being at the bottom of the Atlantic. Yet Yenzer was proving a reluctant assassin, demanding more information and upping the contract price to $3,000.

Meanwhile a retrial had been scheduled for Holzapfel's arms hijacking case (the first conviction had been quashed on a technicality), and it would almost certainly result in a hefty prison sentence. The prospect did not appeal to Holzapfel, who consequently responded favourably when Peel suggested he leave the country. Once again, Peel promised to cater for his financial needs, this time through their dubious investment company. And once again, Peel failed to deliver. What money did reach Holzapfel at his new home in Rio de Janeiro came through in a very slow trickle.

In January 1960, Peel gave Yenzer $500 as a down payment for the murder of Holzapfel, and added that he might have to make the 'hit' in Rio. Yenzer continued to stall.

It was then that another valuable informant joined the Sheriffs' Bureau team. Now that Holzapfel had fled to Rio, ex-cop James Wilber had lost his $20,000 bail money. Generous to a fault, Peel had given Wilber two cheques to cover the deficit, but both had bounced. Now Anderson and Lovern set about using the disillusioned Wilber to lure Holzapfel back from Rio.

Wilber's ploy was to drive a wedge between Peel and Holzapfel which, in the circumstances, was none too difficult. Wilber wrote to Holzapfel, telling him that Peel was running around with his wife (which was one of the few crimes the judge was not guilty of) and that while he, Holzapfel, was strapped for cash in Rio, Peel was raking it in from the investment business in Orlando (which was true). Holzapfel took the bait, and in September he returned to Florida, principally to get Peel to part with some money – that constant source of irritation.

Wilber and Yenzer took Holzapfel to a motel room in Melbourne, a coastal town between Palm Beach and Daytona. The room was wired for sound and next door Anderson and Lovern listened intently, recording the conversation for posterity and the courtroom. Over a period of three days, the two men Holzapfel thought were his friends poured drink into him. And Holzapfel responded by pouring out his heart. As a result, everything about the Chillingworth case was now down on tape, including Peel's involvement.

When Anderson and Lovern decided that they had heard enough, they burst into the room along with two armed deputies. Holzapfel was in no fit state to resist arrest and was dumped in jail, where he attempted to slash his left wrist with a razor blade.

Peel was quickly arrested and tried to bargain for immunity, but State Attorney O'Connell refused to do a deal with him over the murder of Judge Chillingworth. So Peel remained steadfastly silent.

Implicated by Holzapfel in both the Harvey and Chillingworth murders, Bobby Lincoln was more successful in his bargaining and, in exchange for immunity, testified against Peel at the disgraced judge's murder trial in March 1961. Holzapfel too made a formal confession to back up the tapes. He admitted abducting the Chillingworths and when asked why replied, pointing to Peel, 'To save him. I did it for Joe.' Peel protested that the whole charade was a plot to undermine his political career but the jury found him guilty of being an accessory before the fact. They recommended mercy and Joe Peel was sentenced to life imprisonment. It had taken six years of painstaking investigation to bring him to justice.

Holzapfel pleaded guilty to the Chillingworth murders. Before sentencing him, Judge Russell O. Morrow said: 'You and your cohorts participated in a crime or crimes which were gruesome, vicious, cold-blooded, premeditated, designed, the likes of which the history of Florida has never seen ... it was not just a man's life that was taken when Judge Chillingworth was taken. Judge Chillingworth had been a circuit judge for thirty-two years and a county judge two years before that. He was a man of honour, a wise jurist, and in a sense a bulwark in this county and in this state against lawlessness. It not only shook this county and this state, but this nation to have a man who was the emblem of law enforcement, decency and justice taken away. And Mrs Chillingworth, a kind person, who for aught but this court knows had no enemy in the world. And her only trouble was being present.'

Holzapfel was sentenced to the electric chair but later reprieved. While languishing in prison awaiting trial, he told a reporter on the *Palm Beach Post*: 'I knew I could beat the Chillingworth rap if I lied and went along with Joe. Certainly nobody would have believed Bobby Lincoln's story if the two of us had stuck together. But I'd had enough.'

3

One That Got Away

Apart from the elimination of the intended target, an additional objective in any contract killing is to ensure that the hirer remains anonymous and therefore undetected. Professional gangsters like Al Capone had no cause to worry on that score – his henchmen knew that if they even contemplated 'talking', they too would end up with a bullet in the head. But in the more 'amateur' type of contract killing, with which we are principally concerned here, the risk of identification for the paymaster is considerably greater. Very few escape justice. The hit man usually tells all: sometimes because the contract has not been honoured financially, or because he is unwilling to face the consequences alone; sometimes as a genuine expression of remorse.

But one hirer who did get away with murder was the person who sanctioned the killing of former fashion model Barbara Gaul near Brighton in 1976. It is a case which has been open to much speculation, but although the man who pulled the trigger was convicted, no charges have ever been brought against its architect.

As first the lover and then the wife of millionaire property tycoon John Gaul, Barbara Gaul had enjoyed a champagne lifestyle. The couple boasted numerous friends in high places. Barbara's life was a social whirl of endless parties enriched with practically everything that money could buy: beautiful clothes, fast cars and Caribbean cruises. What more could a young girl want?

Yet Barbara had humble beginnings. She was born Barbara Peart in the sleepy Norfolk village of Blickling, fifteen miles north of Norwich. At the time of her murder, her father, Sidney Peart, was head gardener at the National Trust Estate at Blickling. She was brought up in the village and attended the local school before heading for the bright lights of London, where her photogenic face and beautiful dark hair made her a natural to become a successful model.

She met a 'sugar daddy' in the shape of John Gaul, and in 1963, at the age of twenty-one, she was named as the 'other woman' when Gaul's third wife, Ann Christine, was granted a decree nisi on the grounds of adultery.

John Gaul was thirty years older than Barbara. He had begun to deal in property before the Second World War but in 1940, when property values dropped, he transferred his interests to engineering. He bought a run-down garage at Crawley on the Surrey-Sussex border and sold it to a multi-national oil company at a huge profit after the war. He was a shrewd businessman. He opened an office above a shop in Croydon, and in 1952 took over a company called Sun Real Estates, which had paid no dividends. By 1962, it paid a fifty-five per cent dividend, with £122,000 trading profit. At the time his various companies were estimated to be worth at least £3 million.

His financial acumen allowed him to move in the highest social circles. He was a guest at Prince Rainier's coronation, at the Prince's wedding to film star Grace Kelly in 1956 and at the christening of their first child. He subsequently stayed with the Rainiers in Monaco as well as entertaining them in England.

Barbara Peart became the fourth Mrs Gaul at North Walsham Register Office in June 1971. When they were not jetting around the world, mingling with the rich and famous, the couple lived in Norfolk, at Northrepps, a picturesque village situated a couple of miles from the coast, just to the south-east of the popular holiday resort of Cromer. Their home was the 17th-century Church Farmhouse, a splendid thatched building which Gaul had bought for his retirement and had extensively modernised.

John Gaul was a generous partner and lavished extravagant gifts upon his wife. Their happiness seemed sealed when their daughter Samantha was born in 1972, but two years later they split up and Barbara Gaul moved into Bottledene, a small, whitewashed, semi-detached cottage at Trimingham, no more than a few miles from Northrepps. Just twenty yards from the cliff edge, it stood on what had once been the main road between Cromer and Mundesley. But erosion had virtually isolated the house and two others from the rest of the village.

John Gaul moved back to Hide-Away House, which stands in the grounds of a 250-acre Elizabethan estate at Lowfield Heath near Crawley. He also had a flat in fashionable Belgravia in south-west London. The marriage split was far from amicable and little Samantha was caught in the middle. There was a dispute concerning custody and the child was made a ward of court. Samantha stayed with Gaul's daughter from an earlier marriage, Antoinette, and her husband at their large, detached home in London Road, Brighton. Antoinette was made the child's legal guardian, and John and Barbara Gaul were both allowed monthly visits.

After she gave up modelling, Barbara Gaul's work as a freelance commercial traveller and demonstrator kept her away from Norfolk for long periods, but when she was at home, she made a point of finding time twice a week to drive over in her little blue N-registered Fiat 126 to check on the welfare of her parents in nearby Blickling. And, of course, she was a regular visitor to Brighton to see Samantha.

By December 1975, divorce proceedings were imminent between the Gauls, and for one reason or another, Barbara Gaul was unable to visit her daughter that month. So it was arranged that to compensate, she should make a two-day visit in January. Antoinette's husband, Julian Tasker, booked Mrs Gaul in for the night of Monday 12 January 1976 at the Black Lion Hotel, Patcham, which was about four hundred yards from their own house, where Samantha was staying.

He later testified: 'I arranged the accommodation for her and told the immediate family – my wife, stepdaughter and Barbara's husband, Mr Gaul.'

Barbara Gaul set off from Trimingham in her Fiat on the morning of the 12th. Arriving in Brighton, she spent the rest of the day with Samantha at the house and then, at around 8.00 pm, drove the short journey along London Road to check in at the hotel.

She parked in the car-park of the Black Lion but as she stepped out of the vehicle and prepared to take her overnight bags from the back seat, a figure emerged from the darkness and shot her twice at close range.

Customers drinking in the hotel heard the shots and rushed out to find her slumped on the forecourt. The first person to reach her recalled: 'She was still conscious but badly hurt. She said, "I have been shot." Someone was running away up Church Hill, alongside the pub.'

Cradled in the arms of her comforter and gasping for breath, she also managed to whisper the address where Samantha was staying. Barbara Gaul was taken to the Royal Sussex County Hospital with serious chest and stomach wounds. Surgeons feared that she might lose her left arm but were able to save it. The weapon used in the attack, a Belgian-made 12-bore shotgun sawn off at both the butt and the barrel, was found a few yards away from the scene of the shooting near the hotel's outside lavatory, where it had been discarded by Barbara Gaul's assailant. Both barrels had been fired.

John Gaul was notified of the shooting at his London flat later that evening. The police immediately set up road blocks and searched the South Downs with dogs. Superintendent Maurice De'Ath, head of Brighton CID, said: 'We have been interviewing members of the family looking for the background, trying to gain information which might provide us with a reason for this happening. It appears to have been an unprovoked attack but there must have been a reason.'

Indeed there must. As the police probed into Barbara Gaul's lifestyle – their investigations included an eight-hour interview with John Gaul at his Belgravia flat – they came up with two theories. One was that the pretty thirty-four-year-old was the victim of a crime of passion, possibly being gunned down by someone with a love-grudge; the other was that she was the target for a contract killing.

They did have one good lead. A 1964 green and white Ford Cortina estate had been seen near the Black Lion on the Monday night. Police were convinced it was the getaway vehicle, and when it was traced to a breaker's yard in Bow, east London, two days later, they quickly rounded up six people on charges relating to the attack. Two brothers were charged with attempting to murder Barbara Gaul – Roy Edgeler, a forty-nine-year-old driver from Bow, and his brother, thirty-four-year-old Keith Edgeler, unemployed, from Waltham Abbey.

Roy Edgeler was a hit man with a heart. When police first arrested him and asked him about the unused shotgun cartridges (only two of the six had been fired), he led officers to a chalk pit just outside Brighton for fear that children might be injured playing with the cartridges. Under a bush near a popular play area, they found some objects wrapped in rags, including four live 12-bore cartridges. Most of the shot had been removed from two of them and the gaps packed with paper, rendering them a good deal less lethal. Unfortunately for Barbara Gaul, the ones that had been used to shoot her had not been similarly doctored.

In February it was confirmed that John Gaul had been suing his wife for divorce. But the hearing of the petition at Norwich was adjourned when Gaul mysteriously failed to appear.

For a while, it seemed that Barbara Gaul would pull through. When she had arrived in intensive care, her blood pressure had been unreadable and her body and clothes were riddled with shotgun pellets. Her left elbow was destroyed. But between a series of major operations, she managed to whisper her side of the story to waiting detectives in a few brief moments each day. Handed a sketched plan of the Black Lion Hotel car-park, she was able to draw in the position of her car and that of the gunman. She also gave the police a description of the man who had shot her. As her condition improved slightly, she was taken off the critical list and was able to get out of bed, but on 26 March, over two months after the shooting, Barbara Gaul died. The Edgeler brothers were now charged with murder.

Their trial began at Lewes Crown Court on 9 June. Both denied murder. Roy Edgeler confirmed that he had been hired to carry out the shooting but maintained that the contract did not dictate murder. 'I didn't mean to kill her. I just had to hurt her,' he said.

He claimed he was having a drink in a London pub when a man approached him and asked him if he wanted to do a job. 'He told me there was a woman who somebody wanted hurting. He said: "You will have to give her one with a shotgun." Killing was not mentioned, and if he had said that, I would not have agreed.'

Edgeler's statement went on to describe how the mystery man gave him the home address of a woman at Trimingham in Norfolk, a description of her Fiat car and a brief description of the woman herself. 'He said the job was worth £5,000 when I had done it. He would supply the gun to me the next day.'

Edgeler said he found Mrs Gaul's home in Norfolk and, using his brother Keith as driver, watched her over a period of several months. On one occasion, he followed her from Brighton to her Norfolk home 'hoping to get a chance to do it.' But it was a foggy night and the pair lost her.

Describing the actual shooting, his statement said: 'She was just locking her car door. I just walked up to her about three feet away and I aimed the gun at her from my waist. I had a finger on each trigger. I pulled one of the triggers and it went bang. She screamed and turned towards me. I pulled the other trigger.'

Much as he now regretted it, Roy Edgeler was quite prepared to admit to the shooting, but there was no question of his revealing the identity of the man who hired him. The reason behind this vow of silence was not so much a case of honour among thieves but more sheer terror. For Edgeler was a frightened man. He may have had a lengthy criminal record but it was mostly for minor offences of dishonesty, nothing to compare with this. Quite simply, he now realised he was out of his depth. But at the time when he accepted the contract, he had just been released from prison and was, as he put it, 'skint'. And £5,000 was a lot of money.

His statement underlined his philosophy: 'I have no intention of saying who the man in London is who asked me to do this job because if I do, I am as good as dead.' For good measure, he pointed out: 'I have never dealt with anybody else but that man.'

Mr John Leonard QC, prosecuting, revealed that, in addition to the whereabouts of the remaining cartridges, Roy Edgeler had also shown police the escape route taken by him and his brother that night, as well as a telephone kiosk from where he had unsuccessfully tried to call a number written on a piece of paper. He had subsequently thrown away that scrap of paper and it could not be found.

In his statement, Keith Edgeler, who always referred to his brother as Mick, gave his version of events. He said that Mick/Roy had rung him up and asked him if he wanted to make 'a few quid on the side' by driving him around. 'I did not really want to know, but I was hard up and wanted money. I asked how much and he said, "A lot of money." I needed money to pay off my debts.'

He said that he and his brother had made at least three trips to Norfolk looking for a certain car, and they also went down to Brighton four or five times. They travelled down to Brighton again on 12 January, spotted the car and kept a watch on it for several hours.

He continued: 'I parked up the hill round the corner. Mick had shown me where I had to wait while he was doing the job. Mick got the gun out of the car and hid it in the hedge. I heard two bangs. Next thing I knew, Mick ran up the hill and jumped in and I drove off.'

Keith Edgeler claimed that he didn't even know the victim's name until he read it in the newspapers. He told police that he did not know who had put up the money or why, but his brother had said that his share would be £2,500.

This singular case took another bizarre twist. No sooner had the trial started than it ground to a halt after Mr Justice Willis injured his spine while doing a spot of gardening at the weekend. The new trial started two days later and Mr Justice Wien ruled that this time the Edgelers should be tried separately.

Opening the prosecution case for Roy Edgeler's trial, Mr Leonard repeated that there was bound to be speculation as to the reasons behind the shooting of Barbara Gaul. 'Whoever ordered it must have known her well enough to hate her, and also be aware of where she would be at 8.00 pm on 12 January. The person who knew where she would be was her husband, and he would obviously be close enough to her to have a motive to want to do something to her. It can only be speculation because there is no evidence to prove that, and it is academic because Mr Gaul is not at the present time in this country.'

Roy Edgeler's plea that he had only meant to hurt Barbara Gaul was rendered highly improbable when a firearms expert disclosed that the shotgun cartridges used in the shooting were of magnum type, the most powerful available. In fact they were so powerful that it was not safe to use them regularly in that particular gun. The expert said: 'The gun would probably stand a few such cartridges. If more were used, there would be some danger of the barrels bursting.' He added that the gun was in poor condition and the safety catch was defective, but he found no tendency for the gun to discharge accidentally. The fact that weaker cartridges had been rejected in favour of stronger ones and that both barrels had been fired instead of just the one seemed to blow a hole in Edgeler's case. The prosecution asked: 'Is that consistent with an intention merely to hurt or does it indicate a deliberate intention to kill, to get rid of her?'

However, Edgeler was sticking to his story. Reading a prepared statement, he revealed how he had met his contact in a pub and told him he was short of money. The man, whom Edgeler described as 'a bloke I knew from some years back, a right villain', gave him £20. Edgeler then asked if there was anything he could do to earn 'a few quid'. He made a meeting with me for about a week later and I met him in a car.

'He said: "I have got something. If I tell you what it is, there's no backing out. This has got to be accepted once I divulge it. There is a woman that someone wants seen to. She has got to be hurt and you have to give her one with a shotgun."

'He said he would meet me later but I understood the job was to hurt, not to kill. Killing was not mentioned and I can only assume, as Mrs Gaul has died, that I could be in serious trouble with these people. This has never been my scene, although I admit I have a long criminal record for offences of dishonesty.'

Edgeler maintained that his brother Keith knew nothing of the contract, adding that he employed him only because he was a good driver and he needed somebody he could trust. He then went on to describe how they visited Norfolk and Brighton in search of the victim. By now, he had been given a gun – a .410 with two cartridges. 'One day we were coming back from Norfolk and we stopped by some woods. I thought I would try out the gun. I fired it at a tree and it only knocked off some bark. I was not very impressed with it, and because I did not think I would get my money if I did not do a good job, I told him I did not like the gun. I did not think it would be any good to cause injury and I would be accused of not doing the job properly.'

As a result, he handed over the .410 and was given a 12-bore sawn-off shotgun with six cartridges.

Edgeler talked about the long periods of observing Barbara Gaul. 'I was delaying doing the job because I did not want to do it. I kept making excuses in the hope that the job would be withdrawn. In fact there were at least two occasions when I could have done it without any trouble whatsoever, but I was still hoping the job would be called off.

'Around early January the contact started putting pressure on me and accused me of messing about as it had been dragging on too long without any result. He was quite clearly irritated and I became worried because I could see he was getting a bit upset, and from my knowledge of the kind of person I was dealing with, I reckoned he might eliminate me and put someone else on the job if I did not do the job as soon as possible.'

The pair went over the escape route several times until the fateful day dawned. Roy Edgeler said that he picked two shells at random from the six he had been given, unaware that they were the two most powerful. It really was an unhappy coincidence.

He said he took the gun from a briefcase and hid it by the car-park while Keith parked further up the road. Roy watched Mrs Gaul drive up in her Fiat and a transit van parked next to her.

'I picked up the gun from behind the wall . . . I walked straight up to her and fired a shot. She half-turned towards me with her hands raised and said, "Oh, Oh, Oh." Apart from turning towards me, she did not move at all. I thought I had missed or that there was something wrong with the gun. I was very nervous, trembling.

'It was a very dodgy situation and there were people in the pub behind me who must have heard the shot and would be out in a minute. Because of this and because I thought I had missed, I fired a second shot. I did not intend to hurt her where in fact I did. I intended to hurt her in the left leg only. I had aimed, so I thought, at her left leg and I can only think I missed so badly because I was trembling and also because I was trying to make my escape.'

He then ran to the car and threw the clothes he had been wearing from the window as they made their getaway.

'If I had been instructed to kill her, I would have refused to have done it despite the consequences. I do wish to say I feel truly very, very sorry for the terrible thing I have done and I fully accept responsibility for it having happened. However, I must stress I never intended to kill her. I did not think she would die if all had gone according to plan.'

Again, Roy Edgeler's admission that he had swapped guns because the first weapon with which he had been issued was not powerful enough hardly added credibility to his claim of only wanting to hurt. The following day he changed his plea to guilty.

But Roy was not finished yet. Trembling as he

stood in the dock, he read another prepared statement, this one calculated to allay public rumour. 'I feel that in view of what has been said about Mrs Gaul's husband, John, I should tell this court that although I did not know who my employer was and, indeed, I would never reveal his name even if I did know, I can say from my limited knowledge it was not John Gaul who employed me. Beyond that, I am not prepared to disclose any further matters.'

So that put an end to the speculation about John Gaul's involvement. Or did it?

Roy and Keith Edgeler were both found guilty of murder and sentenced to life imprisonment. Mr Justice Wien recommended that Roy should serve twenty years before being considered for release on parole. Sentencing him, he said: 'I am abundantly satisfied that you intended to kill Mrs Gaul whatever the terms of your contract were. There were many features of this case which point to such a conclusion.'

He went on to underline the fact that Edgeler had tested and fired the original gun, decided it was not a very effective weapon and changed it; that Edgeler had shot Barbara Gaul with both barrels at a range of three feet; that he had aimed at Mrs Gaul's trunk, not at any other part of her body; and that he had meant to kill his victim because he took no steps to avoid identification.

The judge added: 'Happily, the hiring of a gunman to shoot innocent people is a very rare agreement in this country.'

As sentence was passed, Roy Edgeler stood shaking in the dock, hanging his head.

Keith Edgeler, who also had a history of minor

criminal activity and had only been released from jail in July 1975, a month before his brother, was found guilty of murder on a majority verdict of ten to two after the jury had been out for nearly five hours. In his case, the judge gave no recommendation as to a minimum term. Mr Justice Wien told him: 'It is quite apparent to me that you were in this plot from the beginning.'

Roy Edgeler had done his utmost to protect his brother as well as his employer. Ultimately he had failed in the first respect but he continued to maintain a stony silence with regard to who had hired him to gun down Barbara Gaul.

However, the police certainly did not consider the case to be closed and announced their intention of tracking down the moneyman. Despite Roy Edgeler's statement, the finger of suspicion continued to point at John Gaul, and in July 1976, a warrant was issued by Brighton magistrates for his arrest, accusing him of murdering his wife. But the problem was that the tycoon was nowhere to be found. He had put the somewhat aptly named Hide-Away House in Crawley up for sale and had gone to Milan on a business trip. He was now believed to be somewhere in South America. In fact he had left Britain three days after the shooting and had not been in the country at all while his wife was fighting for her life.

The hunt for John Gaul began to rival that for Lord Lucan. In December 1977, a national newspaper reported that he had been seen in Geneva, and the following month the millionaire finally broke his silence and wrote an eight-page letter to *The Sunday Times* to explain his absence.

In his letter, he denied that he had arranged a

contract for his wife's murder but claimed that 'inquiries revealed my wife's nature as the local whore'. He also claimed that his own life had been threatened a few days before his wife was shot and accused the police of threatening to arrest friends and a solicitor who had been asked to reveal his whereabouts. Mr Gaul said he cooperated with police when he was questioned hours after the shooting and when he told them he was going to Milan for a business appointment, they raised no objection.

He explained that he flew to Italy on 15 January 1976, intending to return to London, but instead bought a car and drove to Paris. 'I drove back to Paris and had time to think of what I was coming back to. I decided to take a rest – I am, by the way, sixty-six years old – and see parts of the world I had never previously been to, and I went first to Rio for a bit of winter sun. I travelled there, and everywhere else I have been since January 1976, on my own UK passport, issued to me in the usual way by the Foreign Office in London.'

He added: 'I accept that I may have done some things in my life for which others might criticise me, but nothing that should debar me from getting fair treatment and a fair trial – which I am clearly not going to get.'

The letter contained no indication of John Gaul's whereabouts at the time.

In early April 1978, the elusive Gaul was traced to Malta, and the Foreign Office sent a telegram to the British High Commission there instructing them to request the Maltese authorities to place him under provisional arrest. The request was made under the terms of an extradition treaty between

Britain and Malta. But the Maltese premier, Dom Mintoff, had already warned that anyone wanted by British police would not be returned following the refusal of the British government to allow a Maltese woman, wanted on a forgery charge in her own country, to be extradited from Britain.

While the wrangling continued between the two governments, Brighton magistrates issued a fresh warrant for John Gaul's arrest. Meanwhile, he took the opportunity to marry a fifth wife, another Norfolk girl, his former nanny, twenty-three-year-old Angela Pilch, who had joined the Gaul household a few weeks before the birth of daughter Samantha back in 1972.

Finally, in July 1981, the Maltese formally turned down the extradition request. Three years later, the British police withdrew the warrant for John Gaul's arrest after the Director of Public Prosecutions decided that the evidence available did not justify criminal proceedings against him.

Free at last, in the autumn of 1984 John Gaul returned to Britain from his self-imposed exile, for the first time since Barbara's death, to attend his son's wedding. He said bluntly: 'I did not consider coming back to face the charges because when the time comes to die, I don't want to be kicked to death in a police cell.'

John Gaul's time to die came five years later on a flight to his home in Malta. It seemed that despite the whispers and innuendo, he had after all finally been exonerated of any involvement in the contract killing of his wife Barbara. And whatever secrets he had he took to his grave.

Yet within a month of John Gaul's death, there was one last dramatic twist. Keith Edgeler broke his thirteen-year silence in an interview at Ford Open Prison in West Sussex with a reporter from the *Brighton Evening Argus*. In the course of their conversation, Edgeler told the reporter that John Gaul was 'as guilty as sin'.

Edgeler claimed that he and his brother had been promised £10,000 if they did the job before Christmas 1976, but never received any of the money. He said they were given instructions by Mr Gaul after a rendezvous had been arranged in the car-park of a Newmarket hotel.

'He [Mr Gaul] just walked over to his car, where we had been told to stay, and handed me a note. He was very calm. At that time I didn't know he was John Gaul, but after the shooting he appeared on the television and I recognised him immediately. There was no mistake unless he had an identical twin. Mr Gaul was the only person who could find out about Mrs Gaul's movements. He used to find an excuse to meet her even though they were separated. I suspect the man my brother used to phone was also Gaul, but he never told me that.'

Edgeler said the motive for the killing was not jealousy, as the police had suspected, but that Barbara Gaul was about to sell her story to a newspaper. 'She was about to name names and a number of top people were worried. Pressure was put on Gaul to do something. It was as simple as that.'

We will probably never know whether Keith Edgeler's claims are true. It must be remembered that he had previously testified on oath that he had no idea who had hired him and his brother. Perhaps this confession was an elaborate ruse to throw police off the scent by blaming a dead man. But why bother after all those years? The scent had long gone cold. The only thing that does seem certain is that whoever ordered the murder of Barbara Gaul got away with it – and it didn't cost him or her a penny.

4

The 50-Cent Contract

The summer of 1939 was a terrifying time for the Polish people wherever they lived in the world. Even before Hitler unleashed the full ferocity of the German army to bombard Poland from the air and trample her underfoot with tanks, the citizens of the Baltic port of Danzig, the Führer's most coveted prize, were subjected to a string of brutal attacks. Hundreds of Poles employed in the shipyards were arrested by local Nazis and deported to concentration camps in Germany. Although they were a few thousand miles away from the front line and thus not subjected to the full force of the Nazi jackboot, it was an equally traumatic period for the many Poles living on the other side of the Atlantic. There was the constant fear of what would happen – or might have already happened – to friends and relatives left behind.

In such times of stress and anxiety, it was natural that these Polish emigrés should take comfort from their faith. Even those who had allowed their churchgoing habits to slide flocked back to places of worship to seek solace in religion and pray for their loved ones.

The parishioners of the Polish Baptist Church in Camden, New Jersey, an industrial town in the shadow of sprawling Philadelphia, considered themselves to be particularly blessed. Their pastor was the Reverend Walter Dworecki, a father of three children and a fine upstanding man.

At least, that was how he appeared in church. But in reality this man of the cloth was a thoroughly unpleasant individual who was to commit the most heinous crime imaginable, one that even his most devoted followers were to find hard to forgive. He ordered the murder of his own daughter. And the motive? Sheer greed.

Forty-eight-year-old Dworecki was obsessed with money. He had once been charged with arson for profit but had managed to ride the scandal and pursue his career in the church. Nevertheless, he knew that another indiscretion would almost certainly cost him his job – and that was something he could ill afford.

So he made a concerted effort to convince the good folk of Camden that he was wholly worthy of the position of responsibility that had been bestowed upon him. Since God's house was open to everyone, Dworecki thought it would create the right impression if he practised what he preached and decided to open his own house to one of life's underprivileged souls, a youth by the name of Peter Schewchuk, who originated from Chester, Pennsylvania.

But while Dworecki was busy keeping up appearances, there was an element in his household which was threatening to destroy everything he was working towards: his teenage daughter, Wanda. For Wanda did not behave in the manner expected of a minister's daughter. Far from being quiet and demure and a model of chastity, she was boisterous and unruly and spent an inordinate amount of her time in the company of boys. In certain quarters, this was deemed a most unhealthy lifestyle.

Wanda's growing reputation did not go down at all well with the zealots of the Polish Baptist Church. Word of her adventures soon spread and there was a good deal of muttering behind her father's back. Eventually it reached the point where the secretary of the congregation threatened that unless the girl began to mend her ways, the church would be looking for a new pastor.

This was a potential body-blow for Dworecki, and one which he was adamant he could not let happen. Since he believed there was precious little hope of his being able to tame Wanda, he decided that an infinitely more practical solution would be to have her eliminated. It wasn't as if he particularly liked the girl, anyway. And to make it an even more attractive proposition, it would be nice if he could make a tidy sum of money out of his daughter's death. With Walter Dworecki, charity did not begin at home.

So no sooner had the secretary issued her threat than the minister took the first steps to ensure that Wanda's behavioural problems would be a thing of the past. He insured all three of his children for $5,000 apiece, but in Wanda's case he added a special double-indemnity clause, making her death by accident or murder worth an extra $1,000. Thus a dead Wanda was suddenly worth a highly acceptable $6,000, sufficient to satisfy even Dworecki's avarice. He could therefore solve his financial worries and be rid of his troublesome daughter in one fell swoop.

It was one thing wishing Wanda dead but quite another effecting her demise. It would clearly be inconceivable for a man of his social standing to contemplate doing the grisly deed himself – no, it was preferable by far to recruit the services of a couple of young tearaways. He met plenty in his line of work, and with Wanda's dubious character, it was only to be expected that she would associate with such types. Her murder would simply be dismissed as a lovers' tiff. An additional advantage was that if the case ever came to court and his hired hoodlums 'grassed', he would surely still be in the clear. After all, who would believe the word of a pair of no-hopers against that of a respected man of the church?

With these considerations uppermost in his mind, Rev. Dworecki approached two local youths, Alexander Franklin and John Popolo, in April 1939. He paid them $50 to kill Wanda – Dworecki was not exactly generous with his cash – and, being low on principles and high on poverty, they accepted.

But with contract killers, as with everything else in life, you get what you pay for. And $25 apiece bought incompetence. At first everything went according to plan. The pair abducted Wanda in their car and pummeled and choked her before throwing her unconscious out of the speeding vehicle on a quiet country road twenty-five miles outside Camden. If she was not dead by the time they hurled her out, they reasoned that the impact on landing would finish her off. And in such a secluded spot, there were unlikely to be any passers-by hurrying to her immediate aid. But Wanda was made of stern stuff and she survived the ordeal. The minister was not pleased, especially since he had paid out $50 for nothing.

The only consolation for Dworecki was that no evidence emerged at that stage to link him with the crime. Still, he remained hell-bent on his daughter's destruction. He may not have at first succeeded but he was determined to try, try and try again. Even the pitiful sight of her battered and bruised body did not move this man of stone.

Seeking a more reliable assassin, his thoughts turned to his former lodger, twenty-one-year-old Peter Schewchuk, who was now working as a carnival roustabout, a glamorous name for what was essentially a fairground worker. Schewchuk's wages were meagre and he was always on the lookout for anything that would bring in extra money. And as Dworecki was to discover, that included murder.

Reluctantly concluding that if he paid Schewchuk more, there was a better chance of him doing the job properly, Dworecki promised a purse of $100. However, lest Schewchuk think that Dworecki was about to change the miserly habits of a lifetime, the pastor drove a hard bargain. Learning from his previous experience, after which he had finished $50 out of pocket, Dworecki gave him just a 50-cent advance on his $100 fee.

Dworecki hired Schewchuk at the start of August 1939, as the storm clouds were gathering over Europe, and emphasised that he wanted the job done as quickly as possible. On the evening of 7 August, Dworecki instructed his daughter to meet Schewchuk, who was after all an old acquaintance, on a Camden street corner.

Amazed that her father was actually encouraging

her to go out with boys, Wanda complied. Anyway, she had always quite liked Schewchuk. But it was to be Wanda Dworecki's date with death.

The pair met as arranged and Schewchuk bought her a soda drink for ten cents. They got along fine, and Schewchuk took her to a lonely lovers' lane on the outskirts of town. With Wanda at her most vulnerable as she anticipated his tender embrace, Schewchuk strangled her and bludgeoned her to death.

Notified by Schewchuk that his mission had been carried out successfully, Dworecki contacted the local police later that night and reported his daughter missing. The following day, the body of eighteen-year-old Wanda Dworecki was found lying in a patch of weeds near a cemetery, eight blocks from her home.

The pastor feigned horror at the discovery. He prayed for his daughter's soul while his loyal parishioners offered words of condolence in his hour of grief. Even those who had occasionally been given cause to doubt his integrity rallied round to support him in the wake of Wanda's bloody and heinous murder. The killing shocked the whole of Camden. Parents kept their daughters indoors and few youngsters ventured out after dark for fear of being seized by the murderer that lurked within their midst. The police department were left in no doubt that the culprit had to be caught before he struck again.

Had they known then what they were to learn later, the residents of Camden would have realised that their fears were groundless. Peter Schewchuk was no serial killer. He was, to coin a phrase used by those who were soon to invade Poland, merely obeying orders.

As he led his congregation in prayer at the Baptist Church, Rev. Dworecki had good reason to feel content with his efforts. But that old failing which blights so many of those who hire contract killers surfaced again here: the reluctance to pay up. Tight-fisted to the last, Dworecki came to the conclusion that there was no need to keep his part of the bargain. Schewchuk could hardly go to the police and complain about not having been paid for carrying out a murder.

So he left Schewchuk to smoulder. And smoulder he did. He was bitter at the fact that the only money he had been paid for the killing was fifty cents – and he had spent ten cents of that on buying Wanda her last drink. So his net profit was a pitiful forty cents. Even in the poorly paid world of the fairground that was hardly worth killing for.

There was something else preying on Schewchuk's mind. He regretted murdering Wanda. His conscience gnawed away at him and his resentment towards Dworecki increased by the minute, until finally, on 26 August, Schewchuk surrendered to the police and told them everything. To the disbelief of his flock, Rev. Walter Dworecki was arrested two days later and accused of hiring Schewchuk to kill in a murder-for-profit scheme. The charge against Dworecki was one of first-degree murder.

The partners in crime were arraigned on 29 August and both tried to plead guilty, knowing that under New Jersey law, a plea of guilty would make them ineligible for the death penalty. But Judge

Gene Mariano refused to accept the plea and ordered them to change it to one of not guilty.

Dworecki was really in a spot now. He had confessed all to the police in the hope of saving his neck, but with his exit door firmly closed, he decided that his only possible means of salvation was to retract the statements he had made to detectives and claim that they had been made under extreme physical duress. There was still a good chance that a jury would believe the word of a minister against that of the police.

The trial of Walter Dworecki began in Camden in September 1939. Peter Schewchuk's trial was to follow later, mainly because he was the principal witness for the prosecution.

Dworecki's plan was simple. He would claim that everybody was lying except him. So when Schewchuk testified that he had killed Wanda on Dworecki's instructions, the defence counsel immediately set about further tarnishing the youth's character. Dworecki tried to claim that Schewchuk had killed Wanda when she resisted his advances. Then, referring to the time when Schewchuk lived with the Dworeckis, the pastor said that he had been forced to banish him from his home on learning that Schewchuk had been spreading malicious, scandalous stories about Wanda. Being a God-fearing man, and only desiring to clear his daughter's good name, Dworecki said he then asked Schewchuk to return and accompany Wanda on a trip around town during which the young man would formally recant all the blasphemous gossip. That was Dworecki's explanation for the arranged meeting between Schewchuk and Wanda on the evening of 7 August, and also for the fifty cents he had given Schewchuk on the night his daughter was killed.

As for the signed statements he had made to the police, Dworecki claimed that the confession had been forced out of him by brutality.

His trump card – indeed, his only card – should have been his dignity and composure as a man of God. If the jury perceived him as a person of high morals without a stain on his character, they might just believe the pack of lies he was telling them. So it was essential that Dworecki created a good impression in the witness box if he was to escape the electric chair. Unfortunately for him, he allowed the real, mean Walter Dworecki to shine through all too frequently. For interspersed with uncontrollable bouts of sobbing, guaranteed to win any juror's heart, were shouting matches as he ranted and raved. This was scarcely the behaviour expected of someone of his standing in the community.

Even if Dworecki had somehow managed to convince the jury that both Schewchuk and the police were for some reason plotting against him, there was still the damning matter of the extra $1,000 on Wanda's insurance policy, money which, the prosecution maintained, was 'to pay for killing her'.

On 5 October, the jury of seven men and five women found Rev. Walter Dworecki guilty of first-degree murder. As the verdict was announced, Dworecki paled visibly and he was hardly able to stand as he was called to the bar by Judge Clifford A. Baldwin.

The judge announced: 'You have been convicted by a jury of your peers and must be sentenced to death in the electric chair.' He then asked Dworecki whether he had anything to say.

Dworecki, still shaken by the verdict, stammered: 'Well, I'm not guilty of that.'

The judge concluded: 'May God have mercy on your soul.'

As the murderous minister was led away to face the consequences of his sins, two female members of the jury were said to be on the verge of fainting.

By March 1940, Dworecki's homeland had been overrun by the Germans but he was never to see the outcome of the war. On 28 March, he spent an hour in prayer with the Rev. John B. Oman, chaplain of the New Jersey State Prison at Trenton, and then walked to the death chamber. A few minutes after 8.00 pm, Dworecki was strapped into the electric chair. The two ministers prayed together for one last time before the electric current surged through Dworecki's body.

On 2 May, Peter Schewchuk was also found guilty of murder and sentenced to life imprisonment by Judge Baldwin.

So in this instance the man who carried out the contract killing escaped with a prison sentence while his hirer paid with his life. In the case of Rev. Walter Dworecki, it was no more than he deserved.

5

Miss Marlene

Almost without exception, the currency in contract killings is hard cash. It is the only language understood by all parties. But Marlene Lehnberg planned a different method of payment to her hired hit man Marthinus Choegoe: she promised him a radio, a car, sex – and a new artificial leg.

Dubbed the 'Scissors Murder' by the popular press, the case was a sensation in South Africa in March 1975. The trial made front-page news every day and crowds jostled outside the courthouse just to get a glimpse of the two defendants. For they were the oddest of odd couples: a pretty nineteen-year-old white former Sunday school teacher and an impoverished coloured cripple. No wonder their exploits created such a stir. Rarely in the annals of crime have there been two less likely partners. But the overwhelming desire to kill can make for the strangest bedfellows.

Marlene Lehnberg used to be such a nice girl. She came from a respectable home in the highly desirable Constantia suburb of Cape Town, where her parents were regular churchgoers. Friends remembered her as a quiet girl whose most outrageous activity was crocheting.

In 1972, at the age of sixteen, Marlene left home

and started work as a receptionist in the orthopaedic workshop of Cape Town's Red Cross Hospital. There she was taken under the wing of forty-seven-year-old father-of-three Christiaan Van der Linde, a technician in the orthopaedic department and, to all intents and purposes, a perfectly happily married man.

They first became friendly in the February of that year. As a young girl in her first job, she was glad of the help, advice and support of one of her superiors. Initially, so Van der Linde was later to testify, his relationship with her was purely 'fatherly', but within a year it had developed into something stronger. Marlene was no longer the girl fresh out of school. She had become a young woman of quite stunning beauty, so much so that she was seriously considering a career as a model. Van der Linde, nearly twice her age, was naturally flattered by her attention. In April 1973, the affair became intimate.

The lovers would meet virtually every day, at lunchtimes and also after work, when he would give her a lift back to the boarding-house where she was staying. One of their favourite courting spots was a secluded common, a haven of anonymity. He would then go home to his wife and family.

It goes without saying that this arrangement suited Van der Linde down to the ground. He was enjoying the best of both worlds – a loving family at home and a passionate affair with a beautiful girl at work. As far as he was concerned, everything was just fine, provided his wife Susanna remained in the dark about what was going on behind her back five days a week. Van der Linde was deter-

mined to keep his two lives separate, and for that
reason he and Lehnberg never met at weekends.

Christiaan Van der Linde thought he knew
exactly what he was doing. Lying and deceit
became second nature as he made sure that Lehnberg and Susanna never overlapped. He had a
powerful personality, bordering on arrogance, and
Lehnberg was later to claim that he had some sort
of control over her. Van der Linde encountered no
difficulty in cold-heartedly switching from one
partner to another. To him, the affair with Lehnberg
was nothing more than a bit of fun, a massive ego-
boost in his middle age. He certainly did not love
her and had no intention whatsoever of leaving his
wife for her.

However, he seriously miscalculated Lehnberg's
feelings. She may have had the body of a woman
but at heart she was still young and impressionable.
And while Van der Linde continued to treat her as
merely his plaything, an attractive executive toy to
be picked up and discarded at will, she became
increasingly infatuated with this image of the
urbane, mature, older man. When she bared her
soul to him and declared how she felt, he simply
fobbed her off with meaningless platitudes, a catalogue of insincerity designed to keep her happy
until their next session of lust. The trouble was that,
in her naïveté, Marlene Lehnberg believed them.

Over the next year or so, her love showed no
signs of abating – in fact, quite the opposite. She
convinced herself that it was only a matter of time
before Van der Linde left his wife and set up home
with her.

Nevertheless she was aware that their relationship was not actually going anywhere. All she had

to cling to were a few vague promises. Just as Kathleen Calhaem was later to tire of spending just a few moments a week with Kenneth Pigot, so Marlene Lehnberg became frustrated at seeing Christiaan Van der Linde only when it suited him. She wanted him all to herself. She wanted to marry him. And she thought the only person in her way was Susanna Van der Linde.

Although it had by now begun to dawn on her that Van der Linde was not going to break up the marital home, Lehnberg could not bring herself to do the sensible thing and finish the affair. She was too deeply in love for that. No, she decided that if Van der Linde would not end his marriage, then she would.

In June 1974, using the name Marlene Pietersen, she wrote to thirty-four-year-old Marthinus Charles Choegoe, a cripple of mixed race whom she had first met when he was a patient at the orthopaedic workshop. He had only one leg, having lost the other above the knee in an accident in October 1972. An artificial leg had been fitted at the Red Cross Hospital. Choegoe lived in a slum area of Cape Town with a woman named Elizabeth Isaacs. They had been together for nine years and had two young children, although they were not legally married. With apartheid then at its most offensive, life for non-whites in South Africa was a miserable affair. And since Marthinus Choegoe's already slim work prospects were further hindered by his physical handicap, he and Elizabeth led what was very much a hand-to-mouth existence.

Having the skin colour that brought with it all the privileges and power, Lehnberg had come to the conclusion that if her lover could exercise some form of mystic hold over her, then there was no reason why, with her consummate beauty and single-mindedness, she should not be able to control weaker men. The unfortunate Marthinus Choegoe was to be her first guinea-pig.

In her letter, typewritten to make any subsequent detection more difficult, she wrote: 'Marthinus, if you are clever you can still earn good money.' She asked him to meet her at the workshop. Attracted by the suggestion of anyone offering him money, Choegoe took little persuading.

Lehnberg had decided that one viable way of ending Van der Linde's marriage was to have his wife murdered. This is a chilling thought at any time, but in a girl who was then barely eighteen, it almost defies belief. As yet, she was not sure whether Choegoe was up to the job, and so her first approach was to Robbie Newman, a young engineering student who lived in the same boarding-house as her, Stowel Lodge. She was on good terms with Newman, but it was straining friendship to the limit when she asked him whether she could borrow his Llama pistol to shoot Mrs Van der Linde. He refused point-blank, whereupon she asked whether he would like to shoot Mrs Van der Linde for her. Again he rejected her suggestion out of hand, telling her that it was a stupid idea and that she must be mad.

Perhaps having Susanna Van der Linde killed was not going to be as straightforward as it seemed. Maybe she could be worried into an early grave. In one of her love letters to Van der Linde, Lehnberg wrote: 'You said to me that if anything had to happen to your wife, you would look to me. What is the difference if you divorced her now or waited for a year or two until she died of a nervous breakdown?' So in early September 1974, she set off on a different tack, harassing Mrs Van der Linde with a series of telephone calls, each more explicit than the last. Lehnberg defiantly told her that she was having an affair with her husband, that she loved him and saw him every night. She then challenged Mrs Van der Linde by asking what she intended to do about it.

Much to Lehnberg's disappointment, Susanna Van der Linde's response was to do nothing. Not for one moment did she believe that her husband was having an affair, and she passed off the calls as just some silly little girl being a nuisance.

Lehnberg was livid that she had failed to induce the desired reaction. Three weeks after the first calls, she rang again, this time to arrange a face-to-face meeting with her rival. Mrs Van der Linde simply reiterated her position: in no circumstances was she going to grant her husband a divorce. Like Robbie Newman, Susanna Van der Linde was not as weak as Lehnberg had hoped.

Growing increasingly desperate by the day for some explosion to bring the marriage crumbling down, Lehnberg told Van der Linde at one of their Friday assignations that she was pregnant by him. Even Van der Linde started to realise that things were now getting out of hand and, as a further illustration of where his loyalty lay ('loyalty' perhaps being an inappropriate word in this context), he immediately told his wife of Lehnberg's claim. She told him to take no notice. When Van der Linde relayed this to Lehnberg on the Monday, she said that she had miscarried over the weekend. At the trial, it was confirmed that there had never been a pregnancy.

Although Susanna did not seem to believe any of Lehnberg's stories and was vowing to stand by him, the whole business was now spreading uncomfortably close to home. Furthermore, Lehnberg's behaviour was becoming dangerously irrational. She might soon become an embarrassment to Van der Linde at work. He had a responsible job and did not want his position undermined by the flights of fantasy of a receptionist. He had hoped it would never come to this, but he decided to cool the affair.

Even then Van der Linde was not willing to end the relationship immediately. He wanted a few last weeks of pleasure with his enthusiastic young temptress before he abandoned her for good. He later admitted that he 'was only going to break it off slowly' with Lehnberg. In the meantime, in order to appease his wife and put a little more daylight between himself and his lover, he fixed Lehnberg up with a new job, at a place called Vigus Orthopaedic Services. She left her post at the hospital on 30 September.

Her letters to Van der Linde grew bitter. In one she wrote: 'I gave up everything I had for you. Yet you won't give an inch. You would rather live for the rest of your life with a woman you do not love.'

Her boss, Mr Theron, was a kindly man and she tried to ascertain whether he was weak enough to come under her spell. After she had twice been fined for speeding she wrote to him, brazenly suggesting that he should pay her fines. Mr Theron was not that kindly.

But Marthinus Choegoe was definitely putty in

her hands. For in 1970s South Africa, a coloured man was automatically in awe of a well-to-do white girl, particularly a coloured man with one leg and a white girl with a pretty face and long, flowing hair. With suitable deference, Choegoe always called her 'Miss Marlene'. Describing his relationship with Lehnberg and the power she held over him, Choegoe later testified: 'I felt bewitched.'

Having failed to break up the marriage with startling revelations and realising that Susanna Van der Linde was more than a match for her, Marlene Lehnberg returned to her original plan of murder. Robbie Newman had made it clear that he did not wish to be considered for the job, so it would have to be Choegoe. Hiring a man with a pronounced limp and a marked tendency to fall over might not have seemed the smartest move in the world. And one would not have rated his chances too highly in an identification parade. To be cruelly honest, if Choegoe could hardly stand up in court, nor would his defence. However Lehnberg, in that dominant way of hers, convinced him that he was the ideal candidate as a hit man since he would be the last person in Cape Town the police would suspect. Nobody would think he was physically capable of killing anyone single-handed. As will be seen, he wasn't.

Lehnberg arranged a meeting with him at Rondebosch Town Hall. She gave him the money for his bus fare and told him that she wanted him to do some work for her. She wanted him to kill a woman. She wanted him to 'haunt' the home of Susanna Van der Linde.

By now, Lehnberg was so sure of her hold over Choegoe that she did not think she needed to offer a great deal to persuade him to carry out her commands. But, as a demonstration of good faith, she stole a radio from the room of another lodger at Stowel Lodge, a Miss Ackerman, and presented him with it. To someone of Choegoe's means, a radio was a veritable luxury, but no matter how many gifts she showered upon him – she also threw in her car as bait – it could not mask the fact that he was an impotent and somewhat reluctant killer.

The Van der Lindes lived in Gladstone Avenue on the Boston Estate in the Cape Town suburb of Bellville. It was, of course, a white area, and coloured visitors were decidedly unwelcome. So when Choegoe first called at the house on the pretence of asking for change, Mrs Van der Linde told him she had none and slammed the door in his face before he had time to draw breath. But the call did unnerve the householder, and she went out and bought a dye gun as protection in case the spooky-looking stranger returned.

Lehnberg had given Choegoe her new work number, and when he phoned to report his failure she arranged another meeting for the following week at Rondebosch Town Hall, where she repeated that the woman had to be killed. As an added incentive she promised him that 'they would make his leg better at the hospital if he killed Mrs Van der Linde'. The offer of a new leg was certainly something to consider.

In a letter to Choegoe, after explaining that Mrs Van der Linde's son left for school early in the morning, Lehnberg urged: 'The date is now set for Tuesday 23rd. Wait fifteen minutes and then go to work. Use a knife if it will be better or quicker but the job must be done. If you don't get it right, I'll wring your neck.'

If anything, Choegoe's second visit to Bellville was even less successful than the first. This time he did not even manage to get as far as knocking on the front door. Instead he was so scared that he just hobbled straight past the house.

Another failure brought another meeting and another offer. This time Lehnberg said that if he carried out the killing, she would have sex with him. Would the prospect of getting his new artificial leg over prove irresistible and sufficient to galvanise him into positive and fruitful action? Lehnberg was not prepared to take any chances. Having deduced that, left to his own devices, Choegoe was nothing short of a disaster as an assassin, she decided to give him a helping hand by driving him to Bellville herself the next day. So on 24 October, Choegoe, armed with a hammer he had brought from home, was dropped off by Lehnberg to set about his murderous business. He rang the doorbell but nobody answered. It was another abortive mission. Afterwards, the police found him wandering the streets three blocks from the Van der Linde residence. With that subtle diplomacy for which the South African Police are noted, they strongly suggested that he make a hasty exit from the neighbourhood and additionally advised him never to return. Choegoe took the hint and told Lehnberg that he was finished with the murder plan. But it was not that easy to escape from her wicked web.

It was now apparent to Lehnberg that as things stood Susanna Van der Linde was just about the safest person in the whole of Cape Town. Clearly she could not rely on Choegoe to fulfil the contract alone. She would have to tag along as his accomplice. It was now or never.

On 28 October, she stole Robbie Newman's pistol and handed in her notice at work. She told Mr Theron that she was leaving for Johannesburg at midnight on 3 November, a clumsy effort to establish an alibi for the events she had planned for the morning of the 4th.

If ever she doubted the course of action she was pursuing – and there is nothing to suggest that she did for one minute – Lehnberg must have felt vindicated when at 6.00 pm on 1 November, at their favourite meeting-place on the common, Christiaan Van der Linde finally got round to ending their affair.

Lehnberg was devastated. Yet there was no question of abandoning the plan. Surely if Susanna were out of the way, their romance would resume, and it would be even more wonderful than before with the ultimate prize on offer – a trip up the aisle. But at that point Lehnberg was feeling extremely vindictive. She could have been forgiven for venting her fury on the man she felt had betrayed her but she still loved him too much to hurt him physically. She did, however, express her anger in print. In a letter she wrote to Van der Linde but never posted, she said: 'My Darling – you have ruined me forever. The man I loved so much, whom I could talk to, who meant the world to me, who comforted me, has just discarded me.' The use of the past tense should not be taken to indicate that these feelings no longer existed. No, Van der Linde could not be harmed – it had to be his wife, the innocent party, who would pay with her life for keeping them apart.

More hell-bent than ever on the destruction of Susanna Van der Linde, Lehnberg got into her white Ford Anglia early on the morning of 4 November and drove to Choegoe's ramshackle home in the Retreat area. She reached there at around 7.30 am. Choegoe was not expecting her. He thought he had managed to wash his hands of any involvement in the proposed murder but he had reckoned without Lehnberg's iron resolution. He later said: 'When she arrived at the house, she told me she was packed and on her way to Johannesburg.' He added that she wanted him to be a 'witness'.

Choegoe could still easily have backed out but he seemed totally incapable of saying no to her. And he must have known that he was to be more than a witness when she handed him a gun, loaded with five cartridges, on the way to Bellville.

True to the pattern that Lehnberg had established, Mrs Van der Linde saw off her children and her husband that morning. Last of all she kissed her youngest, her seventeen-year-old son, as he set off for school. He looked back to see her in her blue dressing-gown, going back up the garden path to the house. It was the last time he or the rest of the family would see her alive.

At around 9.00 am, Lehnberg and Choegoe got out of the car and crossed the road to the Van der Linde house. Knowing that Mrs Van der Linde had already experienced one unwelcome encounter with Choegoe and would not open the door to him again, Lehnberg decided to ring the doorbell. When Mrs Van der Linde identified her, she locked the most vicious of her four small dogs, a particularly irascible chihuahua, in a room. In the circumstances, it was a remarkably charitable deed.

The instant the door was opened, Lehnberg flew at Mrs Van der Linde. They struggled through from the front step to the lounge, where Lehnberg ended the contest by hitting her adversary hard on the jaw with the butt of the pistol. The savagery of the blow fractured Mrs Van der Linde's jaw and left her unconscious. But Lehnberg had no intention of finishing her off herself. Now that the victim was suitably immobilised, that became a job for Choegoe. It was not that she was too faint-hearted to deliver the mortal wound, simply that she wanted to make sure that the wretched Choegoe alone suffered retribution in a court of law.

So she ordered her unwilling accomplice to throttle the stricken woman. She gave him the gun and told him to fetch a pair of scissors from an occasional table and to stab Mrs Van der Linde through the heart. With the woman who had stood in her way now lying dead, Lehnberg set about further incriminating Choegoe. She took the dye pistol Mrs Van der Linde had bought after Choegoe's first visit and sprayed green dye over his face and clothes.

Contrary to the line she had spun him previously, Lehnberg knew full well that Choegoe, with his distinctive gait, would soon be arrested. Positively brimming with confidence, she was certain that the police would never be able to link him with her. He did not know her surname and all her letters to him had been typewritten. Besides, any flaws in her argument would surely not be spotted by someone with Choegoe's limited intelligence. In her eyes, it was a matter of white supremacy. Of all the factors in this extraordinary case, it was this blatant bid to put the blame solely on Choegoe's shoulders

– an act perpetrated in the immediate aftermath of the slaying of an innocent woman – that raised Marlene Lehnberg from the ranks of crime of passion to cold-hearted, clinical killer.

The obliging Choegoe duly did as he was told and took both guns from the house. The pair then made their escape in Lehnberg's car, having been in the building for twelve minutes.

As was his custom, Christiaan Van der Linde endeavoured to telephone his wife that morning from work because, he stated, 'we were very attached to each other'. Receiving no reply, he tried again before alerting neighbours and his daughter Zelda. The latter was immediately concerned for her mother's welfare and went round to the house, arriving at about 1.00 pm. Because the front door key was not hidden in the garden, she knew her mother must be at home. However, all the doors and windows were locked. She went to phone her father from a neighbour's house. Having been informed that he was not at work – suspecting something sinister, he too was on his way to the house – Zelda peered through a window and saw her mother lying dead in the lounge, next to the piano. Van der Linde arrived shortly afterwards.

The police found forty-eight-year-old Susanna Van der Linde in her bloodstained nightdress. The scissors, which had pierced her bra and her heart, were discovered cast aside in the house, similarly covered in blood.

Predictably, as Lehnberg herself had calculated, it did not take the police too long to haul in Choegoe. A limping man had been seen in the district and when his house was searched, the police found the two pistols along with the five cartridges. He had not even been bright enough to dispose of them. They also found a piece of envelope spattered with green dye. It had contained a letter from Lehnberg.

Choegoe was arrested nine days after the murder, on 13 November, and wasted no time in either confessing to the killing or implicating 'Miss Marlene'. He said: 'She told me to throttle the woman. When she was dead, she gave me the revolver and then told me to get the scissors, which were lying on a table near the telephone, and to stab the woman three times through the heart.'

The pair stood trial at Cape Town Supreme Court in March 1975, the culmination of South Africa's most dramatic murder case for years. Hundreds gathered outside every day with a full house crammed inside the courtroom itself, all eager to see at first hand the face of this monstrous young girl. Lehnberg gave them little opportunity, hiding her eyes behind dark glasses throughout the proceedings.

She pleaded not guilty, insisting that she had not been in the house on the morning of the murder, in direct opposition to Choegoe's testimony. But evidence showed that a cripple could not have overpowered the victim alone, particularly since there had been a running fight in the area between the front door and the lounge. It would have been impossible for Choegoe to have kept pace with such a healthy woman by himself. The prosecution pointed out that the reason why Lehnberg had felled Mrs Van der Linde was to incapacitate her so that Choegoe would be physically capable of completing the task. Lehnberg's letters to Choegoe were traced back to her via her typewriter face, and her macabre missive imploring him to use a knife 'if you think it will be better or quicker, but the job must be done', was deemed to be definite proof of incitement and premeditation. Lehnberg was not as clever as she had thought.

It transpired that after the murder Lehnberg had sent Christiaan Van der Linde a telegram and a letter from Johannesburg. He had destroyed the letter without reading it. When it was his turn in the witness box, Van der Linde gave a poor account of himself, appearing aloof and unfeeling. Nevertheless it was not he who was on trial.

Lehnberg and Choegoe were both found guilty of murder. When Mr Justice H.A. Diemont sentenced them to death, saying that there were no extenuating circumstances, scenes of hysteria broke out in the courtroom. Women inside and outside the court screamed and cried while two men in the public gallery fainted and had to be carried out.

The teenage killer expressed no remorse to the police, just relief, 'as though a weight had been lifted from my mind'. But there was considerable public outrage at the sentences, and in July the case came up for appeal. There the Appellate Division of the South African Supreme Court in Bloemfontein took a rather different view to the trial judge. It ruled that there were extenuating circumstances for both defendants, citing the source of the gruesome deed as Christiaan Van der Linde. Consequently, the death sentences were reprieved, and Lehnberg was jailed for twenty years, Choegoe for fifteen.

They may have avoided the death penalty, but both Marlene Lehnberg and Marthinus Choegoe were left with plenty of time to reflect that people

with dominant personalities can be very dangerous
to know.

6

The Chalk Pit Conspiracy

At dusk on the evening of 30 November 1946, Walter Coombs was walking his black and white collie dog along the North Downs near Woldingham. His route took him to a disused chalk pit on Slines Oak Road, which led off the main thoroughfare between Croydon and Westerham, a short distance north of where the M25 now scythes through the Surrey countryside. It was a desolate spot, so inhospitable that even courting couples shied away from its environs. Since few people ventured that way, Walter Coombs was not expecting to encounter any form of human life, past or present, on his stroll that evening.

Usually the presence of sheep in the area obliged Mr Coombs to keep his dog on a lead, but on this occasion he unleashed the hound near the chalk pit and allowed it to roam free. While the dog made the most of its rare taste of freedom, its master used an ash tree some yards from the pit as a windbreak to light his pipe. As circles of smoke spiralled gently into the cool evening air, Coombs whistled to his dog. Seeing that the animal was paying no attention to his commands but was instead scampering back and forth along the pit edge, barking furiously, Coombs went to investigate the reason for his dog's anxiety. Peering into the chalk pit below, he spotted what looked like a heap of old clothes lying in a narrow drainage ditch at the very foot of the incline. Out of curiosity, he decided to take a closer look. His discovery prompted him to flee the scene with great haste in search of a policeman.

Lying inside the clothes was the body of a young man, aged about thirty-five, his face purple. Tied loosely around his neck was a noose entwined with a dirty piece of green cloth.

By the time the police arrived in force at the chalk pit it was already dark and their examination had to be carried out by lamplight. Dr Eric Gardner estimated that the victim had been dead for some forty-eight hours. Early prognostications suggested suicide. Yet, strangely, although the ground at the bottom of the chalk pit was awash with mud, the dead man's shoes were clean. He had clearly met his death elsewhere before being dumped in this watery grave. One theory was that perhaps he had hanged himself from a nearby tree and been discovered by an innocent passer-by who, wishing to distance himself from the affair, had cut down the body and tossed it into the trench. Unlikely indeed, and rendered impossible by the fact that not only did the rope around the deceased's neck show no signs of having been cut but also that there were no trees in the vicinity with branches of a suitable height from which he might have suspended himself. In addition, there was no indication of rope strands or fibres from the green cloth on any neighbouring tree bark. The case was beginning to take on a more sinister demeanour.

Dr Gardner's autopsy confirmed that asphyxiation was the cause of death. The shape of the rope burn around the victim's neck indicated hanging as opposed to garotting. There were also a number of minor bruises about the body, notably one to the forehead which was not actually visible on the surface.

Meanwhile, at least the police had one concrete lead. In the dead man's pockets they discovered a war-time identity card, naming him as thirty-five-year-old John McMain Mudie. Inquiries revealed that since being demobbed Mudie had been working as a barman at the Reigate Hill Hotel, some twelve miles from his final resting-place. He had last been seen alive two days previously at around 5.00 pm, leaving the hotel for his half-day off.

Interrogation of the hotel management and staff revealed that Mudie had been working there for several months and was generally regarded as a model employee, a quiet individual who kept himself to himself. His previous landlady, a Mrs Evans in Wimbledon, confirmed that he was a thoroughly reputable lodger. He had only been with her for six weeks before being offered the job at the hotel. She had been sorry to see him go. Thus a picture emerged of a handsome man, apparently popular with all who came into contact with him. So why should anyone want to kill him?

The police appeal for information about the case brought forth two gardeners who, walking home from work on the afternoon of the 27th, the day before the last-known sighting of Mudie alive, had spotted a man loitering suspiciously for several minutes at the edge of the chalk pit. He had simply been staring down into the pit. On seeing them, he had suddenly dashed to his car, which was parked behind some trees, and reversed off at great speed. The witnesses remembered that the car was a small, dark saloon, either a Ford or an Austin, and that the numbers on the registration plate were 101.

In Mudie's room at the Reigate Hill Hotel, detectives unearthed what at first seemed to be an innocuous letter, but one which was to prove of the utmost significance in leading them to his killers. It was from a firm of solicitors and was addressed to Mudie's former lodgings, asking him to pass on some cheques to a Mrs Byron Brook, the director of a property company, who was staying in the same house. Mrs Evans told the police that Mrs Brook had been the guest of a woman friend, whose flat took up the entire second floor, for around ten days. A further letter, from the same solicitors, addressed to the hotel in Reigate, urged Mudie to return the cheques immediately. Mrs Evans was unable to throw any light on the matter and added that as far as she was aware, Mudie and Mrs Brook had only met once, a chance encounter on the stairs.

Puzzled by the cheques – Mudie did not even have a bank account – the police went to interview the firm of solicitors who had sent the letters. They said they had been acting on the instructions of the chairman of a property company who had recently moved to 5 Beaufort Gardens, Kensington. His name was Thomas Ley.

Sixty-six-year-old Ley had a colourful, it not chequered, past. In New South Wales, Australia, he had been the Hon. Thomas Ley, Minister for Justice, whose impassioned pleas on behalf of Prohibition had earned him the nickname Lemonade Ley. However, a bribery charge plus the suspicious deaths of

Police leave the office in Mildenhall where Christopher Nugent was gunned down.

Kathleen Calhaem, the spinster spurned.

Julian Zajac, Calhaem's hired killer.

Shirley Rendell, victim in the Calhaem case.

American miners' union boss Tony Boyle interrogated by newsmen in the wake of the Yablonski murder and accusations of vote-rigging.

Paul Gilly *(centre)* is escorted from court after testifying about his part in the killing of Joseph Yablonski.

Silous Huddleston, Paul Gilly's
father-in-law.

The Yablonski's home in Clarksville, Pennsylvania.

Thomas John Ley, instigator of the
1946 Chalkpit murder.

John Buckingham *(right)* leaves the Old Bailey in tears after
Ley had been sentenced to death.

The rotten apple in the Big Apple –
New York City Police Lieutenant
Charles Becker.

Herman Rosenthal, the gambler
killed on Becker's orders.

Herman Rosenthal's widow.

Lt. Charles Becker leaving Sing Sing
with his wife and lawyers as he
fought to escape the electric chair.

Millionaire John Gaul.

Floyd Holzapfel, the hired killer of
Judge Chillingworth and his wife.

two business associates, who happened to be barring his progress at the time of their deaths, brought his political career to an abrupt halt. Ley returned to England in 1929, followed a few weeks later by his long-time mistress, Perth JP's widow Mrs Byron Brook, whose real name was Maggie. The pair had first met when they were both forty. Initially the relationship had been sexual, but for the previous decade Ley had been impotent, and he was now also grossly overweight.

In spite of the fact that nothing physical had passed between them in ten years, Ley remained insanely jealous of anyone he saw as tampering with Mrs Brook's affections. Mrs Brook continued to live with Ley (who was then still residing in Knightsbridge Court) in the quieter role of housekeeper and companion. She had a daughter who had married a man named Barron and had gone to live in Wimbledon. When the daughter was taken ill in May 1946, Ley suggested that Mrs Brook should go and care for her son-in-law. Thus she came to stay at Mrs Evans' guest-house.

In her absence, Ley was eaten away with envy. At 10.00 pm one night in early June, he telephoned Mrs Brook and accused her of having sexual relations with her son-in-law. Ley arrived in a car four and a half hours later and insisted that the poor woman return with him to Knightsbridge. Of course, Mrs Brook was not remotely interested in her son-in-law. She, like Ley, was sixty-six and, by all accounts, did not look a day younger.

Nevertheless Ley remained convinced in his vivid imagination that something was going on and visited Mrs Evans, telling her that Mrs Brook had asked him to take her away because she was being pestered by three men in the house. He demanded the name of the other male tenants and Mrs Evans duly obliged. Among the names she provided was that of the unfortunate John Mudie, although she did state quite categorically to Ley that she thought it highly improbable that Mudie had been sleeping with Mrs Brook since they barely knew one another. However, it later became known that Mrs Brook, in total innocence, had once remarked that Mudie had beautiful eyes.

Some while later, Mrs Evans received another visit from Ley. On this occasion he was more contrite than blustering, saying that he wished to apologise to Mudie. The landlady helpfully gave him Mudie's new address in Reigate.

Ley, who was in the process of moving into 5 Beaufort Gardens, was still torn between whether he should take out his venom on Barron or Mudie or both. He opted for Barron first. One day the son-in-law received a phone call requesting his presence at tea with Mrs Brook at Beaufort Gardens. Fortunately for him he was suspicious, and before setting out he checked with Mrs Brook, who knew nothing of any such invitation. Ley and his hired ruffians were left waiting in vain.

As frustrated by his inability to see off his imaginary love rivals as he was by his inability to have sex, Ley homed in on Mudie and, in an effort to establish a link between him and Mrs Brook, had the cheques, which required her counter-signature, sent to Mudie for forwarding. Naturally Mudie had no idea where Mrs Brook was staying and eventually returned the cheques to the property company. Following the second solicitors' letter, Ley visited Mudie in person, and was apparently sufficiently satisfied that the cheques had been returned to offer his apologies.

But Ley's surface deeds and his innermost thoughts were operating on different planes by now. Beneath his outward remorse, he resolved to teach Mudie a lesson and recruited the services of John Lawrence Smith, a foreman joiner who had been working on the renovations to 5 Beaufort Gardens. Smith in turn introduced Ley to John William Buckingham, a former boxer who ran a car hire business, a man who, according to Smith, could be relied upon to 'keep his mouth shut'. At a clandestine meeting, Ley told Buckingham that Mudie was an evil blackmailer who had been troubling a lady of his acquaintance. Consequently Mudie had to be lured to London and forced to sign a document pledging not to trouble the lady again. The idea was that Mudie would then leave the country. Smith and Buckingham did not query the finer details. After all, Ley had promised them both more than a year's salary.

Of course, the success of Ley's plan depended upon Mudie being brought back to Beaufort Gardens, and for this purpose, Mrs Lilian Bruce, a friend of Buckingham's, was employed as decoy. Posing as a lady of some wealth, she invited Mudie to serve as bartender at a bogus cocktail party in London. He accepted. Meanwhile Smith hired a car, a Ford 8, number FGP 101, and on 27 November drove down to the chalk pit at Woldingham from where he made his hasty departure after being spotted by the two passing gardeners. The following day, Mrs Bruce headed for Reigate in a chauffeur-driven car with Buckingham's son at the wheel. Mudie was duly collected and driven to

Beaufort Gardens, followed all the way by Smith and Buckingham senior in a second car. Just before they reached their destination, the pursuers overtook the first car to be ready to join Ley in providing a welcoming committee. Arriving at Beaufort Gardens, Mrs Bruce let Mudie in by a side door. She then left with Buckingham's son, unaware of the fact that she had just lured a man to his death. The next time she saw Mudie it was in a newspaper photograph reporting his murder.

Even nearly fifty years after the event, it is still not clear precisely what happened at 5 Beaufort Gardens that evening. What is known is that as Mudie entered the house, Smith and Buckingham threw a rug over his head and the blameless barman was then shoved into a front room and trussed up with a clothesline which Buckingham had bought for the purpose. Mudie was also gagged with a green French polisher's rag and spluttered: 'You're stifling me.' At this point, either Smith or Buckingham replied, 'You are breathing your last.' Smith later testified that the comment was 'only said in joking form' and 'was done to frighten this man.' Buckingham claimed he then left, having been given £200 in one-pound notes by Ley. Buckingham's fee for the job was £170, the remainder going to Mrs Bruce. Buckingham was told not to contact Ley again.

But Smith remained at the house for another fateful ten minutes. He insisted that when he left with his £200, Mudie was still very much alive. What is undeniable is that some time that evening Smith or Ley, or both, handed out a beating to Mudie and that one of them then strangled him with the noose. The body was subsequently driven out to Surrey and dumped at the bottom of the chalk pit, where it lay for two days until it was discovered by a man and his dog.

On tracing the letters in the dead man's possession back to Ley, Detective Sergeant Frederick Shoebridge set about interviewing the former Minister for Justice. He maintained that the business with the cheques had been a misunderstanding and that he had wrongly assumed that Mudie had known of Mrs Brook's whereabouts. It was as simple as that.

But the police were not as simple as that, and they decided to carry out some discreet checks on Ley's background. They uncovered the bitter jealousy and the accusations levelled by Ley against the three young men all living in the same house at Wimbledon, each branded with having had sexual intercourse with old Mrs Brook. Detectives became increasingly convinced that the roots of Mudie's demise lay not in any property dealings but in the wicked obsession of Thomas Ley.

The evidence against Ley began to accumulate. The green cloth entangled in the noose was found to have been ripped from a French polisher's rag found at 5 Beaufort Gardens. And a pick-axe discovered at the chalk pit, where it appeared to have been used for partially filling in the trench, was also traced back to Ley's house. Its purpose there had been for mixing concrete during the refurbishments to the building, which Ley was having converted into flats.

It was abundantly obvious, however, that such an obese, unhealthy figure as the 22-stone Ley could not have overpowered Mudie single-handed, let alone carried the body any distance, either from a house to a car or from a car to the chalk pit. If, as seemed likely, he was behind the murder, he must surely have been joined by hired accomplices.

Scotland Yard had now been called in and the inquiry was headed by Detective Chief Inspector Philpott, a no-nonsense guardian of the law who was not likely to be daunted even by Ley's well-practised legal mind. Philpott began to contemplate the possibility that Ley's hired hands were unaware that Mudie was to die that night. He released the victim's name and photograph to the newspapers in the hope that they might prick a conscience.

The strategem paid instant dividends. Within hours of the story appearing in the press on 14 December, just two weeks after the discovery of the body, John Buckingham walked into Scotland Yard and confessed to a senior officer that he had been paid £200 by Ley to kidnap John Mudie. Of Mudie's abduction at Beaufort Gardens, Buckingham said: 'There was no fight or struggle. We just shut the door on him. Ley paid me the money and I left as fast as I could.' Buckingham added that a few days later he had been told that Mudie had signed a pledge and had left the country with £500 which Ley had given to him.

Smith was soon hauled in for questioning and his statement largely tallied with Buckingham's. He maintained that he had left Mudie bound and gagged and alone in the house with Ley.

In his statement, Smith said: 'John [Buckingham] "jumped" him along the hall from the room and into another smaller room, where we were going to keep him prisoner until he had signed the confession, and after that we were going to put him in a car and see him to the airport.'

But he claimed that when Mudie was taken to the other room, he tripped and Buckingham fell on top of him. 'John picked him up and sat him in a swivel chair where Ley had told us to put him. John then asked me to look for a gag. I found a French polisher's rag to use. John pulled the rug off Mudie's head and I tied the gag round his mouth, just so he couldn't shout. He could breathe OK.'

For his part, Buckingham refuted some of Smith's points, denying that Mudie had ever tripped or that a gag had been used.

Philpott was now ready to confront Ley. Believing that his years of professional expertise naturally gave him the upper hand in any dealings with the police, Ley simply denied everything, saying that Smith and Buckingham had invented the whole ludicrous story because they obviously harboured some kind of grudge against him.

The police still felt they had insufficient evidence, but Smith's cause took a turn for the worse when the hired car with the telltale number-plate was linked to him. He was promptly put into an identity parade and one of the gardeners picked him out straight away. However, the other selected somebody else altogether. Yet the fact that Smith had been seen at the chalk pit before Mudie's disappearance was pretty damning evidence and a clear indication that, contrary to his statement, he knew Mudie was to die.

The Director of Public Prosecutions allowed Buckingham to turn King's Evidence with a guarantee of immunity and Ley and Smith were duly charged with murder.

The trial opened on 19 March 1947 at the Old

Bailey with the Lord Chief Justice, Lord Goddard, presiding. The prosecution case was led by Mr Anthony Hawke and Mr Henry Elam while Smith was defended by Mr Derek Curtis-Bennett and Ley, who could afford the finest counsel in the land, had Sir Walter Monckton leading his defence. Both Ley and Smith pleaded not guilty.

Smith conducted himself poorly in the witness box, coming across as a man with something to hide. He insisted that Mudie had been alive when he left him and that he did not believe Ley intended to kill the captive. However, he admitted that he had not really cared what happened to Mudie.

Ley did neither himself nor his counsel any favours by sticking steadfastly to his story. He denied all knowledge of Mudie or of any conspiracy to kill him. He was prepared to accept the overwhelming evidence that Mudie had been brought to his house and that he had been tied up there and gagged with a cloth taken from the building. But he maintained that he knew nothing of the events of that evening. Ley offered no plausible alibi for his whereabouts on the night of the murder, and his testimony was a combination of bluster and rambling irrelevance. He was virtually challenging the police to link him with the crime.

As we have seen elsewhere in this book, the one area which invariably causes the downfall of those who hire contract killers is the pay-off. To his credit, Ley was not an employer who defaulted with the payments, but he did have to explain away the missing money from his bank account. Both Buckingham and Smith testified that Ley had paid them each £200 on the night, all in one-pound notes. And Ley's bank records revealed that shortly before the

28th he had withdrawn sums of £250 and £300 in one-pound notes.

When questioned about the withdrawals, Ley said they were to pay for house furnishings. And the reason he had not paid by cheque, he said, was that his suppliers had asked for cash. Yet curiously for such a businesslike individual, he had no receipts for either transaction. In spite of the gathering gloom, Ley remained confident that there was no direct evidence to connect him personally with Mudie's death. And he was even more optimistic that, when it came to the crunch, the jury would accept the word of a former national Minister for Justice above that of two members of the working class.

In contrast, the one witness who emerged with her reputation intact was Mrs Brook, who turned out to be a kindly lady with a gentle disposition, hardly the epitome of a woman at the centre of a brutal crime of passion, although quite what she ever saw in Ley is beyond comprehension.

Much of the trial was taken up with a dispute between the two chief medical witnesses as to how exactly John Mudie had died. Dr Gardner thought that the bruises on Mudie's body were the result of a beating whereas Professor Keith Simpson, the Home Office forensic pathologist, inclined towards Smith's testimony that the injuries were consistent with a stumble, followed by one of Mudie's attackers falling on top of him.

The mark on the dead man's neck strongly pointed to death by hanging rather than strangulation but in neither of the rooms at Beaufort Gardens in which Mudie had been kept was there an object suitable for suspension. Even the hat-pegs in the hall were the wrong height. The theory was therefore put forward that while Mudie was bound and gagged in the swivel chair, someone standing behind him had pulled the noose upwards, tightening it automatically in the process.

Enlarged police photographs of Mudie's neck revealed a straight line which formed a base to the angle of suspension just below the left ear. This, the experts agreed, proved beyond a shadow of doubt that the noose around Mudie's neck had been tightened before being lifted. In the first place, the rope had been held tightly in a horizontal position. Then it had been lifted and held aloft for two or three minutes to cause death by asphyxiation. Clearly this was not a feat which the victim himself could have accomplished and so suicide was categorically ruled out. It was murder made to look like suicide. All in all, it was a most unusual hanging.

As if there were not already sufficient imponderables to this case, the defence threw a further spanner into the works by introducing as a witness one Robert Cruikshank, an ex-convict who had been living in Switzerland. Prior to that, in 1929, he had been in Australia and therefore his path may well have crossed with Ley's, although he insisted that he was not acquainted with the defendant. The reason for his plea of ignorance soon became all too clear.

Cruikshank, a thoroughly disreputable character, claimed that he had flown from Switzerland to England on the afternoon of the murder to conduct some illicit smuggling business. With time on his hands before the flight home, he said he decided to call on Ley, whom he knew only by reputation. He hoped that Ley, as a wealthy native of that country, might be able to fund his return to Australia.

He said he arrived at Beaufort Gardens at 8.00 pm but found the house in darkness. As an alternative method of raising money, he decided to burgle it and broke in via the basement. There he saw a man tied to a chair. Conveniently, Cruikshank's lighter failed at that very moment and so when he went over to the man and pulled on the rope, presumably in an attempt to release him, he could not really see what he was doing. He then thought better of freeing the captive and fled the premises.

Lord Goddard asked him if he was confessing to having killed the man but Cruikshank replied that it was only a possibility. Clearly Cruikshank's testimony contained more holes than the average colander. Why should he seek help from a person he had never met? Why would any self-respecting burglar even contemplate releasing somebody who could then walk straight out and hail a passing policeman? And why did he suddenly flee empty-handed? Above all, Cruikshank's statement that he had merely pulled on the rope was wholly at odds with the forensic evidence, which proved conclusively that the noose had been lifted in a suspended position for at least two or three minutes.

It was highly unlikely that Cruikshank had ever been in the house that night. Far more plausible was the belief that his story had been concocted to make Mudie's death appear accidental and thereby to allow Ley off the hook. Perhaps Ley had offered him a handsome recompense for such a tale.

Lord Goddard expressed similar misgivings and in his summing-up he drew the jury's attention to the possibility that Cruikshank had been bribed in order to confuse the prosecution with the theory that Mudie had met an accidental death.

The trial lasted for four days and the jury took under an hour to reach their verdict. Both Ley and Smith were found guilty of the murder of John Mudie. They were sentenced to be hanged.

Ley complained that the judge's summing-up had been biased but his subsequent appeal failed.

So the case which had begun with a head in a noose looked like ending in a similar manner. But Ley's performance at the trial had revealed a streak of insanity in his obsessive jealousy. Accordingly, while awaiting execution, he was examined by three members of a Medical Board of Inquiry. They ruled him to be insane to the point of paranoia in the strictest medical sense. On 5 May 1947, just three days before he was due to be hanged, Ley was reprieved and sent to Broadmoor Criminal Lunatic Asylum.

This left Smith to face the music alone. He had clearly not been the driving force behind the murder, and indeed it was never proved that it was he who had actually tightened the noose. But the fact that he had been positively identified as being at the chalk pit prior to the abduction made his involvement undeniable. However, in the circumstances, it was only fair that the Home Secretary should also reprieve Smith, and his sentence was commuted to penal servitude for life. Ley was clearly mad but had been sane enough to arrange murder. To have spared Ley, the evil mastermind, but send his hired hand, Smith, to the gallows would surely have been unjust.

Thomas John Ley's reprieve was short-lived, for on 24 July 1947, less than three months after he escaped the noose, he died in Broadmoor of a brain haemorrhage. Rarely has justice been more poetic.

7

You Won't Get Me, I'm Part of the Union

Ambition and greed can be potent allies. As we have seen with Joe Peel, even the judiciary are not above resorting to murder in order to further their aims. So it was with American union boss Tony Boyle who, finding his deviously acquired position and his lucratively paid job under threat from the forces of honesty, resolved to have the source of his irritation eliminated.

The American United Mine Workers' Union had been the subject of whisper and accusation for many years, but such was its power throughout the land that few were bold enough to stand up to it. During the 1950s and 1960s, certain sections of the union were widely suspected of using intimidatory methods to achieve their goals. Occasionally, these suspicions came to the surface in dreadful manifestations of bullying and attempted murder.

Terror tactics were especially prevalent in the coalfields of Eastern America, around the states of Pennsylvania, Kentucky, Virginia and Tennessee. In 1955, a recalcitrant Tennessee coalowner, valuing his right to freedom of choice, bravely refused to sign a contract with the UMW. His stand was rewarded by a sinister visit from a gang of 100 marauding miners who buried him alive in a ditch. Luckily, the man managed to struggle free but any faith he had in American justice was cruelly shattered when those brought to trial were found not guilty.

The acquittals were seen by some members of the union as proof that they were above the law and the case was the signal for further widespread acts of intimidation and violence by those who thought they could run amok with impunity. Over the next few years, gangs of bully-boys roamed the coalfields, putting the frighteners on anyone who dared to oppose the union or even those who merely wished not to do business with it. Coal tips were burned to destruction, drivers were forced to dump their lorryloads of coal on the road and, in the most extreme instances, so-called 'enemies' of the union were shot.

Matters came to a head in 1959, when a number of mines in Kentucky had to close down following a costly and prolonged strike, one marked by particularly heavy union intimidation. As a result, the UMW was obliged to pay $1.5 million in damages to the mine operators, whose livelihoods had been wrecked by the actions of its members.

One of the prime movers in the 1959 violence was Albert Pass, treasurer of the East Kentucky area branch. By 1968, Pass was rumoured to be plotting the 'elimination' of Ted Q. Wilson, head of a rival union, but this plan took a back seat when Joseph Yablonski announced his intention to clean up the UMW by standing for the presidency.

That year of 1968 was a traumatic one for the American people. While the flower of the nation's youth perished needlessly in Vietnam, at home both Bobby Kennedy and Martin Luther King were assassinated. Of less significance, at least on a worldwide scale, was a huge explosion at a mine in West Virginia in November. On investigating the blast, inspectors of the Bureau of Mines discovered numerous violations of the safety regulations there. But the UMW president brazenly announced in public that the company owning the mine had an excellent safety record. Clearly it was going to take more than a mighty explosion to rock the foundations of the union.

The president was sixty-four-year-old Tony Boyle, a short, combative man with piercing blue eyes and neatly brushed sandy hair. It was an extremely prestigious post, union leaders in the United States wielding considerably more power than their British counterparts. And they were well paid, too. Boyle and his leading lieutenants awarded themselves salaries of $50,000 a year and, on retirement, the bonus of a healthy pension.

Boyle believed in looking after his family and used his control and influence to ensure that they profited from his lofty position. His late brother Jack had owned a mine in Montana at a time when the union forced all large mines in the area which competed with those run by members of the Boyle family to close down. And Tony Boyle's lawyer daughter Antoinette was retained as an official of District 27 on an annual salary of $43,000. Yet District 27 had only 870 miners. Thus corruption was rife in the UMW under Boyle's law.

Understandably enough, having risen to the top, Boyle was in no hurry to relinquish his authority or the dubious perks which accompanied it. Such was Boyle's standing that few would have dared to have challenged him anyway. Even those decent union men who disapproved of the activities of Boyle and his henchmen had seen with their own eyes over the past thirteen years what could happen to those who defied the UMW.

But fifty-eight-year-old Joseph Yablonski, known to his friends as Jock, was made of sterner stuff. He and Boyle had both been senior union members when the previous president, John L. Lewis, had stepped down. Since he had been particularly close to Lewis, Yablonski had expected to be appointed his successor, but to his dismay and disgust, Boyle was chosen instead.

Yablonski had no time for Boyle's presidency. He was an honest soul and strongly suspected that Boyle was embezzling union funds. Disillusioned by the improbity which seemed endemic among so many members of the union hierarchy and in particular by Boyle's reaction to the West Virginia disaster, Yablonski decided to challenge him for the presidency. He saw it as the last chance in his life-time to clean up the American United Mine Workers' Union. Tragically, he was only too right.

The election in December 1969 was a predictably bitter affair. Yablonski stood for change, something which scared the wits out of Boyle and his sup-porters. During the campaign, Yablonski accused Boyle of the misuse of union funds, of nepotism and of not being sufficiently vigorous in the essen-tial matter of promoting mine safety. But in spite of a hard-fought battle, Yablonski lost by 81,000 votes to 45,000. Boyle was re-elected as president.

But Yablonski was not finished yet. Having come this far, he was not willing to take defeat lying

down. Not only did he charge Boyle with using
millions of dollars from union funds to finance his
campaign, but he was also convinced that Boyle
had won dishonestly. He was sure the voting had
been rigged and asked the Federal Labour Department to seize and inspect the ballot papers. His
request was turned down. Yablonski was furious,
calling the rejection 'a cheap trick'. But if it was
humanly possible, he was still prepared to challenge the result in the courts.

The prospect of such a move alarmed Boyle,
faced as he was already with an investigation into
the union's financial dealings as a result of Yablonski's allegations. After winning the election, Boyle
thought he had seen the back of his persistent
adversary but he had reckoned without Yablonski's
determination to see justice done. If Boyle were
now to be stripped of the presidency, one thing was
certain – he would not be the only one to suffer.
His confederates would just as surely be exposed
by the new regime. No more fat salaries, no more
jobs for the boys. The situation did not bear thinking about. There was only one solution: the source
of all the aggravation, Joseph Yablonski, would
have to be removed from circulation.

It was later claimed that Boyle had told his
closest associates: 'We are in a fight. Yablonski
ought to be killed or done away with.'

Words to this effect duly reached Albert Pass,
who sparked off a chain reaction among the union's
top brass. No stranger to plotting murder, Pass
immediately contacted UMW representative
William Prater, with whom he had formerly discussed the removal of Ted Q. Wilson. Pass laid it
on the line to Prater: Yablonski had to be killed.

Prater, in turn, relayed the information to Silous Huddleston, the ageing president of the pensioners' branch of the union in La Folette, Tennessee. Huddleston had been a union stalwart for over thirty years, and in his younger days had been one of the militant thugs who waged a campaign of terror among the coalfields of that state.

Abiding by the union policy of keeping it in the family, Huddleston made overtures to his son-in-law, thirty-seven-year-old house decorator Paul Eugene Gilly. On the face of it, Gilly was a curious choice to enrol in the murder plan. He was a quiet, mild-mannered, industrious man with no criminal record. Yet evidently what the union wanted, the union got, for although he professed to want no part in the conspiracy, Gilly somehow allowed himself to be inveigled into the very thick of it.

Gilly's brief was to find an assassin. The vast majority of law-abiding citizens would have found this an insurmountable task, but what Gilly lacked in experience, he made up for in resourcefulness. He outlined the details to twenty-six-year-old Claude Edward Vealey, a drifter with convictions for burglary.

This stratagem was actually drawn up in the summer of 1969, when Yablonski first announced his candidature and his intention to drive out the union's corruptive forces. Possibly because the wiping out of his sole rival midway through the campaign would inevitably have pointed the finger in Boyle's direction, nothing positive was done until it became apparent that, even in defeat, Yablonski was not prepared to abandon his crusade.

The pair were promised $4,200 each for the

murder, but no amount of money can compensate for lack of expertise. A small-time burglar and a painter were scarcely equipped for a contract killing, but old man Huddleston came to the rescue. He advised them to obtain the necessary guns by breaking into Ted Q. Wilson's house.

Joseph Yablonski was married with three children. Grown-up sons Kenneth and Joseph Jr had moved out but daughter Charlotte still lived at the large detached family home in Clarksville, Pennsylvania. By 18 December 1969, nine days after his election defeat, Yablonski Sr was already becoming concerned for the safety of himself and his family. A series of death threats had led him to consider asking for police protection. So when on that day, the murderous twosome turned up at his house, posing as miners looking for work, Yablonski's suspicions were aroused. This was no dummy run, and had he invited them in, Yablonski would have been killed there and then. But in view of the warnings he had received, he wisely decided against admitting total strangers, particularly ones who behaved in such an edgy manner. Instead he conducted the conversation at the door. Gilly and Vealey considered such a location to be far too visible and were forced to abandon the attempt for the day. However, Yablonski did not forget his nervous visitors and when he later saw their car in the vicinity, he wrote down its licence number.

These men belonged to the bungling amateur brigade of hired killers. Such was their incompetence that they had not even thought to steal a car to transport them on their mission of murder. Instead they borrowed one belonging to Gilly's wife, Annette. It was to prove a costly lapse.

Perturbed not only by the death squad's failure to carry out the hit but also by their lack of composure, Silous Huddleston became increasingly impatient. Pressure was mounting from above. Huddleston was all too aware that questions would be asked if Yablonski stayed alive long enough to make further trouble for Tony Boyle. So he hatched an alternative method for the disposal of Yablonski. Accompanied by Gilly, who was by now in too deep to back out, Huddleston approached a young miner and asked him to dynamite Yablonski's house. The man had no wish to become involved but, at that stage anyway, did not disclose the incident to the police.

With no other option presenting itself, it seemed as if Gilly and Vealey would simply have to try again. Vealey suggested that their chances of success would be maximised by recruiting a third member and put forward the name of another minor burglar, James Phillips. At the same time, the contract fee was raised to $5,200 per head.

It was now essential that Yablonski be permanently silenced as quickly as possible. The next attempt on his life was discussed in a bar five days after Christmas. It was arranged for 30 December, but it was soon apparent that Phillips was more trouble than he was worth and after he cheated Gilly and Vealey over some stolen goods, they seriously contemplated dropping him. He was obviously unreliable, not a man to be trusted even in his dealings with fellow criminals. Consequently twenty-three-year-old burglar Aubron Wayne Martin, known to his friends as Buddy, was brought in on standby. When on the very evening of the proposed assassination, Phillips got hopelessly drunk, Martin stepped in to take his place. The services of Mr Phillips were no longer required.

The snow lay heavy on the ground on the night of 30 December 1969. The American people were still enjoying the festive break between Christmas and the start of a new decade when Gilly, Vealey and Martin set out from Cleveland, Ohio, on the long drive to Clarksville. For a nation which five months earlier had put the first man on the moon, it was a comparatively straightforward journey, but given the hazardous weather conditions and the trio's high state of anxiety, it seemed interminable.

They eventually arrived in Yablonski's neighbourhood just as the church bells heralded New Year's Eve. All was quiet in the chill night air, the snow-capped roofs making it more like a setting for a Disney cartoon than an act of murder. Backing on to a wooded hillside and shielded from the winding road by a row of tall trees, the secluded Yablonski house offered ample scope for anyone wishing to act in secrecy. The three parked the car along the road from the main entrance and waited for the lights in the house to go out. Before going in, they tried to build up their courage by drinking considerable quantities of whiskey and beer. This made them even more careless, to the extent that the empty beer cans were tossed on to Yablonski's lawn.

At about one o'clock, suitably emboldened, they broke into the house. Joseph Yablonski was asleep in bed with his wife Margaret while daughter Charlotte slept in another room. Martin entered Charlotte's bedroom, pointed his .38 at her and fired twice. Nothing happened. In his drunken stupor, Martin had forgotten to release the safety catch. He desperately tried to wrench the catch off but merely succeeded in releasing the magazine instead, sending a hail of cartridges cascading to the floor.

The commotion awakened Charlotte, who screamed, alerting her parents. Joseph Yablonski leaped out of bed and groped in the dark for the shotgun which he had been keeping handy since the death threats. But before he had a chance to put the weapon to use, Martin, his gun hastily reloaded, ran into the bedroom and emptied the magazine into the couple. While Gilly silenced Charlotte by shooting her in the head with a carbine, Vealey fired two more shots into the stricken body of Joseph Yablonski. Vealey later testified to hearing Yablonski making a 'gurgling' sound.

Despite their incompetence, Gilly, Vealey and Martin, who had not been expecting to find women in the house, had left three people dead. They drove back to Cleveland through the heavy snow pausing en route to hurl the murder weapons into the Monongahela River. Their paymasters were pleased with the results – but not for long.

On 5 January, Kenneth Yablonski, worried at not being able to reach his parents by phone, drove over to the house. There he found his father shot through the back of the head and the bodies of his mother and sister nearby. The walls, carpets and bedclothes were saturated in blood.

The police were mystified as to the motive for three such horrific killings. All the telephone lines had been systematically ripped out yet nothing had been stolen. However, the police soon got lucky. Two days after the grim discovery, Martin was picked up on a minor assault charge but proved curiously hostile to relatively routine questions. About his person, he was carrying a list of telephone numbers, among them entries for 'Paul' and 'Claude'.

Meanwhile a search of Joseph Yablonski's papers revealed a car licence number which was traced back to Annette Gilly, the daughter of Silous Huddleston. The police interviewed husband Paul and asked him what he had been doing in Clarksville on 18 December. Gilly's explanation was that he had met a singer named Jeanne and had dropped her off at a festival in West Virginia. It sounded unlikely, but then again the hunched figure of Paul Gilly looked an unlikely murderer.

In an act of gross hypocrisy calculated to steer any hint of blame away from the UMW, Tony Boyle sanctioned the union to offer a reward of $50,000 for information leading to the conviction of Joseph Yablonski's killers. The move backfired, however, for when a customer in a downtown bar overhead Claude Vealey bragging about having been paid blood-money, he immediately reported the conversation to the police.

On 20 January Vealey, who had been steadily drinking away the profits of his night's work, told the police virtually everything they wanted to know about the murders. In addition to implicating Martin, who was already in custody, and Gilly, Vealey advised the police to have a quiet word with Phillips.

It was Phillips who gave what details he knew of the contract and thus the connection with the union began to emerge. Having found the murder weapons in the river and arrested Martin, Vealey and Paul and Annette Gilly, the police questioned

Huddleston. Not wishing to be caught with any dirty money on his hands, Huddleston persuaded a local preacher to look after the remainder of the contract cash. But the union man's hopes of avoiding detection were dashed when the FBI, who had taken over the investigation, heard about the young miner who had been asked to blow up Yablonski's house. The miner said that two men had approached him about the job, and he positively identified Huddleston and Gilly. Now Huddleston, too, was arrested.

Gilly, Vealey and Martin were tried separately. On 22 June 1971 Vealey, who had decided to bargain for his life, pleaded guilty in court at Washington, Pennsylvania, to all three murder charges, saying that a deal had been made between the defendants that 'all three of us would be equally guilty'. In a fifteen page statement read to the court, Vealey outlined how he had been approached by Gilly in the summer of 1969 with a proposal for the killing. He said that Gilly was the link-man with someone called 'Tony' and that it was 'Tony' who had funded the whole operation. Indeed, according to Vealey, part of the reason for the delay in carrying out the contract, was that 'Tony' had been experiencing difficulty in raising the money. Throughout the investigation, the name 'Tony' cropped up time and time again yet at this stage nobody knew his identity.

Boyle remained at large for another nine months, publicly denouncing the smear campaign that was being launched against him in some quarters. He claimed that he and his union had been the victims of 'lies, slander and irresponsible misrepresentations of truth'.

The past finally started to catch up with Boyle in March 1972. On Vealey's evidence, Martin, described by the prosecution as a 'baby-faced killer', had already been convicted of the murders and had been sentenced to death the previous November (this was later reduced to three terms of life imprisonment to run consecutively). Now it was Paul Gilly's turn to stand trial, and when on 2 March he too was found guilty of murder and sentenced to death, his distraught wife Annette decided to speak out in a bid to save her husband's neck.

Annette Gilly sparked off a chain reaction in which all manner of rotten creatures came crawling out of the union woodwork. She disclosed how she had taken photographs of her father shaking hands with Tony Boyle, and when she reported where the pictures had been taken, the FBI were sure that Boyle was the mysterious 'Tony'.

In that same month, Boyle was convicted on thirteen counts of embezzlement of union funds and sentenced to five years in prison. All things considered, it had not been a good month for him.

Mrs Gilly's confession resulted in the arrest of William Prater, the original go-between. By now, even iron man Huddleston was beginning to waver. Infuriated that the union had failed to keep its promise to raise a million dollars for his defence, Huddleston naturally took out his ire on the local treasurer and duly implicated Albert Pass. Huddleston also exposed another union official, David Brandenburg, who had cashed the cheque and forwarded the contract money to Prater.

Prater and Pass were each convicted of participating in the killings and sentenced to life imprisonment but not before, embodying the new union spirit of freedom of speech, they had implicated yet another high-ranking executive, William Turnblazer. Determined that the buck should not stop with him, Turnblazer talked and came up with the name everyone wanted to hear: Tony Boyle. Turnblazer admitted overhearing Boyle order the murder of Joseph Yablonski.

At last the FBI were close to getting their man. Boyle's world was in tatters. Although he was in the process of appealing against the embezzlement conviction, he had been stripped of the union presidency late in 1972 on the grounds that his victory had been achieved by fraudulent means. In the three and a half years since the murders, Boyle had watched his empire crumble. He had considered himself untouchable. He was wrong. Now realising that he was about to be arrested in connection with the killings, he tried to cheat justice by committing suicide. He took an overdose of sedatives but was rushed to hospital in time for his life to be saved.

The poison was pumped out of his system and Boyle was able to stand trial in April 1974 on a charge of conspiracy to commit murder. The chief prosecutor said: 'This was no accidental shooting. It was a cold-blooded, brutal assassination.' At the end of a two-and-a-half-week trial, seventy-two-year-old Boyle was convicted of first-degree murder and sentenced to life imprisonment.

Yet Boyle had one last trick up his sleeve – or at least, his lawyers did. They appealed, and in due course the Pennsylvania Supreme Court ruled that the trial judge had improperly refused to admit testimony that might have helped the defence.

Contract Killers

Therefore, on 17 March 1977, Boyle was released from prison pending a retrial.

Any thoughts of an extended period of freedom did not materialise, however, and Boyle was found guilty for a second time in 1978. He was returned to prison where he died on 31 May 1985.

Joseph Yablonski had long been convinced that Boyle was misusing union funds. But even he could not have suspected that they were partly being used to finance his own murder.

8

Hit Girl

Female involvement in contract killings tends to be restricted to the planning rather than the execution. Even in these days of equal opportunities, women are generally considered to be better at the hiring than the firing.

So a case in a village just outside Oxford in 1990, in which a teenage girl was recruited to carry out a murder, was decidedly unusual. The fact that her nerve ultimately failed her so that she was unable to fulfil the contract will probably merely serve to reinforce the underworld view that hired killing is men's work.

Although the outcome was not fatal, the case was a particularly sad one. The attack had been arranged primarily by a woman suffering from a terminal illness in revenge for her husband's bullying ways. It was really a domestic dispute which got out of hand. It should never have reached the stage where murder was even remotely considered as a solution.

The village of Wheatley sits on the A40 a few miles east of Oxford. Despite the intrusion of the main road, it is a quiet enough spot. But peace and harmony were sometimes in short supply in the London Road home of Terry Reeves and his wife

117

of ten years, Christina, a nurse who was suffering from terminal leukaemia.

Members of the family were to testify that 20-stone Reeves used to hit his three stepchildren, Denise, Stephen and Paul, his nine-year-old Down's Syndrome daughter Sarah, and his wife. It was an accusation which Terry Reeves vehemently denied. Denise left home to marry David Cresswell and it was later said that Paul Reeves, too, had been driven from the family home.

Describing her relationship with her stepfather, twenty-one-year-old Denise Cresswell told police: 'None of us ever got on with him. He hit me, he used to hit my brothers and he hit my sister. He moved in and started throwing his weight around like he owned the place. If I was five minutes late, I was locked in a shed or he used to drag me in and hit me around.'

Christina Reeves twice left her husband but went back both times, mainly, according to Denise Cresswell, because Reeves had threatened to fight his wife for custody of young Sarah if she walked out again.

Whether it was her tragic illness that caused her to act irrationally can only be a matter for speculation but, trapped in a loveless marriage, Christina Reeves seriously began to contemplate doing away with her husband. An added incentive was that Terry Reeves' life insurance policies were thought to be worth in the region of £40,000. While this money was certainly not the principal motive, it would prove invaluable in paying for the hiring of a killer. For Christina there was no question of tackling the job herself.

Her first approach was to her son-in-law, David

Cresswell, a mechanic. She asked him to doctor her husband's car so that it would crash. When he refused, she offered another acquaintance, Gary West, £20,000 of the insurance money to kill Terry Reeves. West wanted nothing to do with the plot either.

Then, in July 1990, Denise Cresswell met 18-year-old Louise Price at a party. Price, who lived on Oxford's Blackbird Leys estate, had had an unhappy upbringing. Her father had kicked her out of the family home when she was just fifteen and so she identified with Denise Cresswell's tales of domestic strife. The more the two girls chatted, the more Price realised that the problems she had had with her father were similar to those Denise was enduring with her stepfather.

The following day, Price was told of the plan to kill Terry Reeves. She was offered £8,000 for carrying out the murder. Price later admitted that she had a 'pathological hatred' of fathers who abused their children. She admitted that she would have liked to have stabbed her own father and saw Mr Reeves as a substitute victim.

Once Price had agreed to assume the unlikely role of contract killer, Denise Cresswell and Christina Reeves settled down to discuss the intricacies of the plot with her. Given the fact that Price was a mere slip of a girl and the intended victim was huge and immensely powerful, a gun seemed the most likely weapon to bridge the weight difference. It is hard to argue with a bullet, no matter how feeble the firer. But this proposition was eliminated on the grounds that Reeves' home was semi-detached in a built-up area and the sound of gunfire would inevitably alert the neighbours. And, naturally, it was of paramount importance that Price be allowed to escape after the murder.

The alternative plan, and the one which was eventually to be adopted, was for Price to stab Reeves to death in what would appear to be a burglary which had gone wrong. The advantage of staging the hit in Reeves' own home was that Christina, who by then was back living with him, would be on the spot to prepare the ground. Indeed, she would actually be lying in bed beside her husband when he was attacked.

Although the scheme as a whole was ill-conceived and haphazard, at least some thought had been given as to how Price was to overpower Terry Reeves. It was decided that his wife would slip a couple of sleeping pills into his late-night drink, thus rendering him drowsy to the point of immobility.

Mrs Reeves' other tasks would be to leave open a conveniently positioned downstairs window so that Price could enter the house, and to switch the electricity off at the mains. This last measure would guarantee that, in the event of anything going awry, her husband would probably not be able to identify his assailant afterwards, and it would also, allied with the sleeping pills, further reduce his capacity for self-defence.

The murder of Terry Reeves was deemed to be a matter of some urgency and so it was arranged for the early hours of 21 August 1990, barely a month after the conspirators had first encountered Louise Price.

It was doomed to failure. Louise Price was no cold-blooded killer. She was a young girl who had allowed her emotions to run away with her. Along with her partners in crime, she should have sensed the folly of the idea at a very early stage and nipped it in the bud before it had the opportunity of progressing so far.

But whatever reservations may have been expressed, the operation was all set to go ahead on the appointed night. Almost immediately, there was a major hitch. Eighteen-year-old Paul Reeves, who was supposed to be driving Price to Wheatley, backed out at the last minute. His girlfriend sensibly talked him out of it. In any case, Paul Reeves had no idea that the object of the exercise was murder – he thought Price was simply going to 'rough up' his stepfather, to 'knock him down a peg or two'.

And so David Cresswell was pressurised into taking his place. He later claimed to be an equally reluctant participant, telling police that although he had heard his wife and mother-in-law talking about the murder plot with Price, he did not think for one minute that they would go through with it. He stated: 'I wish I had just smacked the missus in the nose and said: "No, I am not going." I told them from the start I didn't want anything to do with it.'

Nevertheless, Cresswell did drive Price to London Road, Wheatley, that night. It was two o'clock in the morning when, wearing industrial gloves lent to her by David Cresswell and a dark anorak, Price clambered in through the ground-floor window which Christina Reeves had deliberately left open. Armed with a carving knife and a Stanley knife, one in each hand, she stealthily climbed the stairs and crept into the bedroom where she knew that Christina and Terry Reeves would be lying in bed.

By now, her heart was pounding. As she stood over the motionless, sleeping figure of Terry Reeves, she suddenly lost her nerve. All it needed was a couple of quick thrusts from the carving knife and it would be over. She would be £8,000 richer and Christina Reeves and Denise Cresswell would be rid of the tyrant in their midst. But with the victim at her mercy, she realised she could not go through with it.

As she contemplated abandoning the mission and slipping back downstairs, she accidentally stepped on a creaking floorboard. The noise roused Terry Reeves from his slumbers. Aware that there was somebody in the room, he tried to switch on the light but, with the electricity switched off, the room remained in total darkness.

Now Price really did start to panic – and with good cause. For if a sleeping Terry Reeves unnerved her, a wide-awake Terry Reeves battling for the safety of himself, his family and his property, was a daunting prospect, particularly since the tablets seemed to be having precious little effect.

He scrambled from his bed and tackled the mystery burglar. In the struggle that followed, she managed to stab him several times about the face, arms and hands. Both parties were fighting for their lives.

Price later told the court: 'He started to get up and I lashed out. He started to get up again and I lashed out again and he fell on me. He then tried to twist the carving knife into me, all the while begging his wife to call the police.'

Christina Reeves was in a real dilemma. She did not know what to do for the best. One thing was certain – she could hardly call the police. In the end, she managed to drag her husband off Price. Faced with his wife's inactivity, Terry Reeves staggered downstairs to raise the alarm, leaving a trail of blood in his wake, and was found by neighbours lying in his garden. Meanwhile Mrs Reeves let Price out of the house before calling the police. It had all gone horribly wrong.

Forty-three-year-old Terry Reeves was taken to Oxford's John Radcliffe Hospital to have his wounds stitched. He described his attacker as possibly being as young as fifteen. In the pitch black, he had assumed it was a boy.

The police combed the house and its long gardens. At first glance, the evidence pointed to a burglary. The telephone wires had been pulled out of the wall and some valuables were missing, but somehow it did not add up. How many burglars would bother to switch off the mains electricity? How many burglars would know where it was? Then there was Mrs Reeves' behaviour. Why had she prised her husband away from the attacker? With the raider pinned to the floor by her 20-stone husband, there was ample opportunity for her to have raised the alarm.

Within a day, the collaborators had been arrested.

The trial took place at Oxford Crown Court in November 1991. Louise Price, by then nineteen, and forty-four-year-old Christina Reeves admitted conspiracy to murder, but Paul Reeves, Denise and David Cresswell pleaded not guilty. Denise Cresswell, a mother of three young children, maintained that although she knew of the murder plot, she did not think Price would carry it through.

Mr Anthony King, for the prosecution, described Christina Reeves as the 'prime mover' in the murder plot. He said: 'She obviously wished to divorce her husband and left him for a short time but was persuaded to return because she had no money and she was concerned about the welfare of her eight-year-old handicapped daughter, Sarah.'

Of the struggle in the bedroom on the night of the attack, Mr King added: 'Mr Reeves got from his bed and at that moment Louise Price struck a number of times, using the weapons she had. He grappled with her, pinned her to the ground and she slashed at him. He seized hold of the carving knife and twisted it. Meanwhile, it would seem his wife, rather than come to her husband's assistance as he was shouting for help, stood there, hysterically, doing nothing.'

After a short trial, the jury acquitted Paul Reeves but found Denise and David Cresswell guilty of conspiracy. Christina Reeves was jailed for two years, the judge, Mr Justice Rougier, reducing her sentence because of her illness; Denise Cresswell was jailed for two years and David Cresswell for twelve months. Louise Price was given three years' detention in a young offenders' institution.

Sentencing them, the judge said: 'This was a dreadful crime, a wicked crime. However selfishly and brutally Terry Reeves behaved, and I accept he did behave selfishly and brutally, there is no excuse for taking the law into your own hands in such a monstrous plot as to stab a man to death as he slept in his own bed. You must have taken leave of your senses.'

By March 1992, Christina Reeves, Denise Cresswell and Louise Price were free after the Court of Appeal reduced their sentences. Mrs Reeves and Mrs Cresswell each had their terms cut to twelve

months with eight months suspended, and Price
had her youth custody sentence trimmed to twelve
months. Taking into account the time the women
had served in custody awaiting trial, it meant they
qualified for immediate release.

This whole sorry case was best summed up by
one of the defence barristers at the trial. He
described the murder scheme as 'a lunatic idea with
ridiculous arrangements'. But it was one which,
but for Louise Price's nerve failing her at the vital
moment, could have turned out so much worse for
all concerned.

9

Mother Love

The two young men smiled pleasantly as they entered the room. They sat down in chairs marked A and B. Still they engaged in friendly banter even after a lever had been pulled to release cyanide pellets into a vat of acid beneath their chairs. As the poisonous fumes wafted upwards, their mood changed. 'I can smell it,' said one. 'And it doesn't smell good.' Within ten minutes of entering the room, Luis Moya and Gus Baldonado were dead, executed in the gas chamber at San Quentin.

Three hours earlier on that same day, 8 August 1962, an outwardly respectable woman of about fifty-eight had also sat in the cold steel chair. As if settling down for a prolonged knitting session, she had made herself comfortable before fixing her gaze on the two guards who were strapping down her arms. 'Where is Frank?' she asked sternly. Then she shut her eyes and took her final four deep breaths. At 10.12 am, Elizabeth Duncan was pronounced dead.

The triple execution marked the culmination of one of the most chillingly bizarre cases in American criminal history. It centred around a mother's suffocating love for her grown-up son. When her son found happiness with another woman, the mother ruthlessly hired two hit men to have the poor girl butchered.

Even before she became involved in murder, Elizabeth Duncan's life makes amazing reading. Born Hazel Sinclara Nigh in Kansas City, possibly in 1904 (although her various marriage certificates list a variety of years between 1900 and 1913), she married one Dewey Tessier when she was just fourteen. She had three children by him, all of whom were hastily dispatched to an orphanage. Over the ensuing years, she married at least eleven and maybe as many as twenty men, most of them bigamously.

The majority of these marriages were annulled on the grounds of non-consummation, although she did have a nice line in blackmailing her husbands into support payments. She also specialised in defrauding businessmen, most of whom were too ashamed at their own gullibility to complain to the authorities, particularly since a number of them had been lured into her trap in the first place by false promises of financial rewards.

In 1928 she married Frank Low, and within four months, her son Frank was born. Low died in 1932 but by then she had moved on to her next partner, a Mr Duncan. Since Low was still very much alive when she tied the knot with Duncan, the 'marriage' to the latter was bigamous, a state of affairs which presented her with the opportunity for further trips to the altar. One of these was with a Mr Craig, whose name she retained for her fraudulent financial dealings long after they had parted because he had an excellent credit rating.

Although she flitted between husbands like a moth at a laser show, she was determined to hang on to young Frank. He was the only constant in her ever-changing life.

However, the darker side of her nature manifested itself during her marriage to George Satriano in the early 1950s. Not altogether surprisingly, Mr Satriano's love for his bride diminished somewhat when he learned that she had offered a private detective $500 to throw acid in his face. In the subsequent arrangement, Satriano got a divorce and Mrs Duncan got a Cadillac.

As was her wont, she did not wait for the Satriano divorce to be finalised before marrying again. Her latest beau was Benjamin Cogbill, with whom she was arrested a few months later for prostitution offences. While in the spring of 1953 her beloved son Frankie was studying at law school in San Francisco, by a peculiar irony, Elizabeth Duncan was running a brothel in nearby Santa Barbara. This 'massage parlour', as she called it, was just another of her business ventures – at various times she also owned beauty shops, cafés and a real-estate business.

Following the annulment of the Cogbill marriage, she wed twenty-six-year-old Stephen Gillis, one of Frank's class-mates at law school. She had promised Gillis $50,000 if he would marry her, the proceeds of a non-existent trust fund. In the event, all he ever saw of Mrs Duncan's supposed inheritance was a $10,000 cheque which was capable of bouncing right across to the east coast.

It was probably a relief to Gillis that the marriage was never consummated – nor did the happy couple ever live together – but Mrs Duncan made sure that he remained ensnared by resorting to her old trick of blackmail. She informed him that if he should try to divorce her, she would accuse him of assault, fraud and blackmail, sufficient to render it impossible for him to pursue a legal career (although, curiously, having a mother with a conviction for running a brothel did not seem to hinder Frank's progress). Sensing that he had made something of a miscalculation in marrying her, Gillis fled to join the Marines. But Mrs Duncan was not to be denied. She marched into a doctor's surgery with a pregnant woman in tow. She introduced the woman as Mrs Elizabeth Gillis and got the doctor to confirm the pregnancy. The hapless Gillis was thus forced to send support money to her before he could finally win an annulment.

At her murder trial, Gillis was to say of Mrs Duncan: 'She had a tremendous spell on everybody that she came in contact with, and no matter what lie she told, no matter how fantastic, it was believable.'

Elizabeth Duncan lived with Frankie in Santa Barbara, where he had been born, a prosperous Californian coastal town ninety miles north of Los Angeles. Softly spoken and always immaculately turned out, to those who did not know of her inventive private life she appeared to be just an everyday doting suburban mother. But when those piercing blue eyes narrowed behind heavy horn-rimmed spectacles and that thin little mouth tightened still further, she looked every inch a woman capable of murderous designs.

She surrounded herself with a gaggle of geriatric groupies who seemed in awe of her driving personality. Notable among these was Mrs Emma Short, a stony-faced widow in the first throes of senile dementia.

But of course these hangers-on took second place in her affections to Frank, who admitted that he was 'the apple of my mother's eye'. Having qualified as a lawyer, Frank soon discovered that whenever he was in court, his mother was present too. She would loudly applaud his speeches, hold his hand in court and even vociferously berate the district attorney if Frank lost the case. This behaviour, allied to the fact that Frank had a lisp and was known around the courthouse as the 'Wicked Wascal Wabbit', made him something of an object of ridicule among the legal fraternity of Santa Barbara.

At her trial, witnesses told the court that Mrs Duncan had admitted often sharing a bed with her son. One testified: 'She said that sometimes she would awaken very frightened and she would call to Frankie and that he would come and jump in bed with her and console her or she would go and jump in Frankie's bed.' Frank denied that any such visits ever took place.

But once when Frank was lying in bed, Mrs Duncan turned to Emma Short, who had popped round, and cooed: 'Isn't he beautiful?' She often described him to complete strangers as 'still Mama's little boy' – and he was nearly thirty at the time.

Predictably for one so obsessed with her son, Elizabeth Duncan could not bear the thought of ever losing him. When a doctor treating her for an overdose of sleeping pills pointed out that one day Frank would probably get married, she retorted: 'Frank would never leave me. He wouldn't dare. He wouldn't dare get married.'

On another occasion, she told a doctor's receptionist that if Frank did marry some girl, she would 'get rid of her'. Clearly Mrs Duncan was not a mother-in-law to be taken lightly.

By a supreme irony, when her darling Frankie did meet his future bride, it was Mrs Duncan who unwittingly introduced them.

It started on 6 November 1957 when Frank, for once, dared to stand up to his mother over a beauty parlour she was considering buying. They had a bitter argument which ended in Frank ordering her out of the apartment.

Devious as ever, her immediate reaction was to take another overdose of sleeping pills – not enough to kill her but enough to make Frank feel guilty at treating her in such a manner. That way, she thought, she would soon be able to clasp him back to her bosom once again. She finished up in the town's Cottage Hospital. Every bit as repentant as she had hoped, Frank rushed to her bedside – and promptly set eyes on attractive twenty-nine-year-old nurse Olga Kupczyk. It was virtually love at first sight.

Olga, who had moved south only the previous year from Vancouver, Canada, where her father was a foreman on the railroad, was a quiet, friendly girl who did not seem to have an enemy in the world – that is until she started showing an interest in Elizabeth Duncan's son.

Mrs Duncan was forced to watch the romance blossom from her hospital bed, but once she was back home, she wasted no time in trying to put a stop to it. When Frank was taken ill and Olga sent him a bunch of roses, Mrs Duncan promptly threw the flowers in the bin. After one visit, she told old

Mrs Short that she could have happily broken Olga's leg.

Fearing his mother's reaction, Frank tried to play down his relationship with Olga until, in May 1958, he learned that Olga was pregnant. He braced himself for the impending vitriolic backlash and told his mother that he was contemplating marriage. She was furious and launched into Olga over the phone, raging: 'I will kill you before you ever marry my son.'

Frank had been made to promise that he would not marry Olga without first telling his mother, but he decided to throw caution to the winds and obtained legal dispensation to marry her the following day. He went to extraordinary lengths, more so than the average rock superstar, to keep the details of the ceremony secret. Terrified that his mother would discover his deception, he arranged for the wedding to be kept out of the newspapers but there remained the little matter of how to explain away the immediate post-nuptial period. Frank had to pretend to his mother that nothing had happened and that meant continuing to live with her. As a result, his wedding-night bliss with Olga was interrupted in a somewhat unsatisfactory manner late in the evening when he returned home to Mummy.

This most peculiar practice continued over the following weeks. Frank later admitted: 'I was going back and forth like a yo-yo.'

But Frank had underestimated his foe. Mrs Duncan had found out about the wedding almost as soon as the ring was placed upon Olga's finger. She had merely phoned the hospital and asked to speak to Olga, only to be told by a minion who had not been briefed about the secrecy of the operation that Nurse Kopczyk was packing in her job because she had just got married. Old Mother Duncan's hackles rose so high they were practically in orbit.

Armed with this information, she then embarked on a ferocious war of attrition against the unfortunate Olga. If it had been a boxing match, it would have been stopped in the first round. It was simply no contest. Mrs Duncan was every daughter-in-law's worst nightmare – and a lot more besides.

Her first attack, launched just four days after the wedding, produced an ad in the local paper stating that Frank Duncan would not be responsible for debts contracted by anybody other than his mother. Frank of course knew nothing about the notice printed in his name, but it did not take a shrewd legal brain to deduce that the culprit was his dear mother. Limply, he told her 'not to interfere again'. He might just as well have saved his breath.

Mrs Duncan progressed to regularly harassing Olga in the street and attempted to persuade a local shopkeeper to stop her credit by claiming that she had run up large bills at a department store. In addition, she phoned Olga virtually every day, threatening: 'If you don't leave him alone, I'll kill you.'

It began to dawn on Elizabeth Duncan that words alone were not going to destroy the marriage and so she hatched a hare-brained plot to kidnap Frank in a bid to drum some sense into him. Recruiting the services of the ever-willing Emma Short and another Miss Marple clone, seamstress Helen Franklin, she announced her intention to render Frank unconscious with sleeping pills, take him to

Los Angeles and coerce him into divorcing Olga. The plan reached such an advanced stage that Mrs Short and Mrs Franklin were both to be found lurking in the Duncan apartment one night, all ready to tie Frank up. But when Frank refused to take the pills, the little old ladies' evening of adventure was spoiled. They would have to get their kicks out of watching *Highway Patrol* instead.

Her next idea was even more outrageous. Spinning another web of lies about Olga, she persuaded an ex-convict named Ralph Winterstein, who had been sent by the Salvation Army to wash her windows, to pose as Frank in order to obtain an annulment. She told Winterstein that Frank could not go in person for fear of ruining his professional reputation. So, on 7 August, Winterstein (posing as Frank), Mrs Duncan (posing as Olga) and Emma Short (posing as Olga's aunt – a neat character invention, worthy of any soap opera) went to an attorney's office in nearby Ventura. The case was heard in court that day. But the outcome was not exactly what they had hoped for, and Winterstein was later convicted of perjury.

In a desperate attempt to escape her tormentor Olga twice moved apartments, but Mrs Duncan always managed to track her down. One evening, she followed Frank when he went to visit his wife and created an unholy scene. She sought the aid of the apartment manager, insisting that Frank and Olga should be evicted because they were living in sin. Just when she seemed to be winning officialdom round to her viewpoint, she overstepped the mark and began raving: 'She is not going to have him. I will kill her, if it's the last thing I do.'

Discussing the means of murder with her peren-

Mother Love

nial confidante Mrs Short in the same way that other folk of their age talk about the weather or the price of tea, Elizabeth Duncan drew up a number of possibilities. She had considered, but discounted, that old favourite of hers, throwing acid in the face, because it would not prove fatal. Even a disfigured Olga could still pose a threat. Another suggestion was for Olga to be lured to Mrs Short's apartment where Mrs Duncan would be waiting with a rope. She would leap out of a cupboard, strangle Olga, hang her in the cupboard and then, later that evening, weigh down the body with a rock and hurl it into the sea.

Mrs Short objected to the proposition in the strongest possible terms – not, however, to the idea of a woman who had done her no harm whatsoever being murdered, but because there was no way she was going to allow a corpse to be hung in her neatly stacked cupboard for hours on end.

Thwarted once again, Elizabeth Duncan turned her thoughts to hiring someone else to do the job for her. Indeed, she had already approached an old neighbour, Barbara Reed, to help take care of Olga. Mrs Reed was to hurl acid into Olga's face whereupon Mrs Duncan would smother the newlywed with a chloroformed blanket. The pair would then truss Olga up, drive her to the mountains in Frank's car and throw her off a cliff. The fee for the killing would be $1,500.

Mrs Reed said she would think about it but instead told Frank. He confronted his mother, who insisted that Barbara Reed had been lying. Frank did nothing.

Mrs Duncan continued to shop for a contract killer. She scoured the streets of Santa Barbara in

search of a murderer with the same cool businesslike detachment she used on an expedition to buy
her week's groceries. The only difference was that,
as far as she knew, killers didn't give stamps.

After a couple of other abortive approaches,
including one to the reluctant Winterstein, she
remembered Diane Romero, whose husband
Rudolph had been successfully defended on a
drugs charge by Frank. Reasoning that the Romeros
were in debt to the Duncan family, Elizabeth spun
a yarn about Olga blackmailing Frank. She urged
Mrs Romero to visit Olga's apartment at 1114
Garden Street and kill her. Mrs Romero did go to
the flat, but was greeted by Olga like an old friend.
It transpired that she had once been a patient of
Olga's in British Columbia.

Although for some reason she decided not to
impart news of the death plot to her former nurse,
Mrs Romero did at least have the good grace to
go cold on the deal. So Mrs Duncan approached
Rudolph Romero, offering him $2,000. When he
appeared less than enthusiastic, she threatened to
have him thrown back in jail. Although he was one
person who could not be intimidated by her, he too
failed to notify the police.

Finding a contract killer in Santa Barbara was
proving more awkward than Mrs Duncan had
imagined. Then on 12 November she struck lucky.
With the ubiquitous Emma Short in tow, she set off
on a trip to the seedy side of town, to a dubious
establishment called the Tropical Café. Its name
was a glamorous misrepresentation of what was
essentially nothing more than a grubby beer-house.
Her motive for seeking out such an unlikely water-
ing-hole was that Frank had recently defended the

café's owner, Mrs Esperanza Esquivel, and her husband, Marciano, on charges of receiving stolen goods. The case against Mrs Esquivel, an illegal Mexican immigrant, had been dismissed, but Marciano had pleaded guilty. He was in jail awaiting sentence and an application for probation, both of which were scheduled for five days' time. The Esquivels, therefore, were in dire need of Frank's services.

As the two old ladies approached the Tropical Café through the notorious Mexican quarter of Santa Barbara, Mrs Duncan was confident of success this time. She only had to glance at the mean-looking individuals loitering on the street corners for confirmation of her optimism. They all gave the impression that they would cheerfully slit their own mother's throat for a fistful of dollars.

The establishment was devoid of customers that morning until the pair sat down and ordered coffee. Mrs Duncan wasted no time in introducing herself to Mrs Esquivel, who was serving behind the counter, nor indeed in getting down to the real reason for her visit.

'You will remember me, I'm sure,' said Mrs Duncan. 'My son Frank defended you and your husband.'

'How can I help you?' replied Mrs Esquivel, a shade suspiciously.

'My daughter-in-law is blackmailing me,' replied Mrs Duncan. 'And I have just had another call from her. She wants $1,000 and if she doesn't get the money, she will throw acid in Frank's face.' Then leaning forward, she confided: 'Do you have any friends who would help me get rid of her or get her out of the way?'

Contract Killers

Mrs Esquivel considered the matter for a second. 'There are some boys, but I don't know if they will want to talk to you or not.'

'Could you please arrange for us to meet them?' requested Mrs Duncan.

'Come back tomorrow afternoon and they will be here.'

At around 2.45 the following afternoon, the women returned as arranged and were introduced to two young Mexicans, twenty-one-year-old Luis Moya Jr and his best friend, twenty-six-year-old Augustine Baldonado, known to all as Gus. Both were unemployed, and in exchange for meals they worked at the Tropical in a fairly haphazard capacity, sweeping up or occasionally tending the bar. Baldonado also lived with the Esquivels.

Moya, who hailed from San Angelo, already had convictions for burglary and needed money to buy drugs. Baldonado too was a drifter and an ex-con, and their paths had crossed during a rare, brief spell of employment at a Santa Barbara restaurant. Despite their criminal backgrounds, neither had ever contemplated anything as serious as murder. But neither of them had ever before met anyone quite like Elizabeth Duncan.

'This is Mrs Duncan, the one who wants to talk to you,' announced Mrs Esquivel. Moya and Balonado, who had been cleaning the café, sat down at the bar with their would-be employer while Mrs Short was dispatched to a back table. The boys drank Pepsi-Cola and listened intently to Mrs Duncan's proposition.

'How much?' asked Moya.

'$3,000,' ventured Mrs Duncan.

'Make it $6,000,' pressed Moya.

'All right,' agreed Mrs Duncan, '$3,000 up front and the remainder afterwards.'

'We will need a car, weapons and gloves,' added Moya, who had assumed the role of spokesman for the two killers. 'We haven't got much money so could you give us something right away?'

Mrs Duncan reluctantly acceded to the request before getting down to the main item on the agenda: how to dispose of her daughter-in-law. She enthusiastically provided a list of possibilities involving items already in her possession from previous plots – the rope, the sleeping pills and the acid. Virtually all that was missing was the lead piping and the candlestick.

As well as giving them the precise location of Olga's apartment, she also filled them in on the prospective victim's work routine – Olga had returned to nursing, at the St Francis Hospital.

Moya later testified: 'So I finally suggested the plan we all agreed to. If we saw her coming or going from work and if there was nobody who would see us, we would kidnap her off the street, or we would go up to the apartment and force her there, you know, open the door – not force her to open the door, but have the door opened for us and force our way inside and perhaps knock her out or something and then tie her up, get rid of all her clothes or part of her clothes and make it appear that she was on vacation or something. And we were supposed to have taken her to San Diego and then transferred her across the border and done away with her in Tijuana.'

'But you'd better watch out,' warned Mrs Duncan. 'She's a pretty strong girl. She might put up quite a fight.'

Moya said he knew where he could lay his hands on a gun but rejected the offer of Mrs Duncan's car as a means of transporting Olga to her grave, sensibly deciding that the fewer links between he and Baldonado, who had no obvious motive, and Mrs Duncan, who had every motive, the better.

Mrs Duncan then went to fetch their down payment. She said she was going to the bank but instead went to a nearby pawn shop and emerged with $175 in exchange for her rings. This she gave to Moya in the kitchen of the café. He and Baldonado had thus agreed to murder for an advance sum of less than £55 each.

Moya and Mrs Duncan settled on a code word, 'Dorothy', to be used at all times. Before leaving, she emphasised that she meant business, claiming that she had already paid $1,000 to someone else but that person had let her down.

'There is no need to worry,' said Moya. 'We will do it.'

As she and Mrs Short tottered out of the Tropical, Mrs Duncan was thoroughly pleased with life. 'I think we've got a real bargain with those two,' she enthused. What made it a particularly good deal was the fact that Elizabeth Duncan had absolutely no intention of paying them much more than their paltry advance, even when the job was completed. It will have been observed from her life of bigamy and blackmail that she was pretty low on principles.

However, as many before them, Moya and Baldonado were taken in by her powers of persuasion. They did not believe for one moment that she would try to double-cross them. Moya later said:

'We did trust Mrs Duncan. We thought her word was good, as we made good ours.'

They certainly kept their side of the bargain – and quickly. Having hired an old cream-coloured Chevrolet and borrowed a .22 pistol from a friend, Moya and Baldonado called at Olga's second-floor apartment on the evening of 15 November 1958. Getting no reply, they resolved to try again two days later.

It was around 11.00 pm on the 17th when Baldonado arrived at the cramped bungalow of Moya's friend Virginia Fierro. After the usual friendly banter, Baldonado summoned Moya to his feet. 'Well, let's go take care of business,' he said in a matter-of-fact manner. With that, the pair departed.

Olga had two visitors that evening, old nursing colleagues from the Cottage Hospital who had come to cheer her up. They left at 11.10 pm. Twenty minutes later, the Chevrolet drew up outside the neat two-storey apartment block on Garden Street. Moya went upstairs alone, leaving Baldonado slumped in the back seat, pretending to be Frank Duncan.

Luis Moya knocked on the door of number 1114. Olga answered, wearing a pink dressing-gown.

'I have brought your husband home, Señora,' he said. 'I met him in a bar and he's pretty drunk. He has quite a large amount of money with him and he told me to bring him home. He is downstairs in the car but I need help to bring him up.'

Although Frank was not a heavy drinker, nor was he likely to associate with customers like Moya, Olga replied without hesitation: 'Sure, I'll help you bring him up.'

She went down with Moya and, seeing the figure

in the back which she presumed to be her inebriated husband, opened the car door.

'Frank?' she queried quietly, not wishing to arouse the neighbourhood.

As she spoke, Moya whipped out his gun and hit her over the back of the head. She was bundled into the car, screaming. The shape in the back seat sprang to life. Baldonado held her down while Moya raced round to the driver's seat and motored off towards the Mexican border.

However, Olga was a restless captive. She continued to scream and struggle and at one point made a grab for the door handle. Baldonado tried to silence her by throttling her, but to no avail. So when they reached a stop sign on the deserted streets, Moya turned round and dealt her several more blows over the head with the pistol. Olga Duncan slumped to the floor with blood pouring from her wounds.

Just as things seemed to be going according to plan, the car began to shudder. It was apparent that they would never make the Mexican border and so they settled for the mountains just thirty miles south of Santa Barbara. Moya said: 'We did go up there until we found a nice little spot to bury her.'

The 'nice little spot' was a ditch off Highway 150. But as they shoved the seven-months pregnant Olga out of the car, they found she was still alive. They couldn't shoot her because the gun had been broken by Moya's earlier attacks so they took turns in strangling her. To make absolutely sure she was dead, Moya brought a large rock crashing down on her head. When they were finally convinced she was dead (Baldonado had been in the medical service and tried to feel her pulse), they began to bury her. The woman whose only mistake in life had been to marry Elizabeth Duncan's son had suffered a lingering, agonising death.

Burying her body in the lonely mountains under the cover of darkness should have been a routine exercise. But they had forgotten to bring a spade. They had no option but to dig with their bare hands until they had made a hole large enough to take Olga's body. As killers go, they had earned their money that night.

On the drive back to Santa Barbara, Baldonado mumbled: 'Let's hope the old lady will pay up.'

'Don't worry,' replied Moya. 'She'll pay.'

Both they and the car were soaked in blood. They ripped out the stained seat covers and the next day took the vehicle back to its owner. It was not exactly the ideal state in which a hired car should be returned, but they explained away the absence of half of the upholstery by saying that they had got drunk the night before and had accidentally started a fire with a cigarette. They promised to fix it properly later. They then bought some ice-cream and threw an impromptu party for Virginia Fierro and her three young children.

Olga's friends from the hospital became worried at being unable to contact her the next day. Frank was alerted and reported his wife missing to the police. There was a theory that, depressed about her crumbling marriage, she might have committed suicide.

Meanwhile Moya and Baldonado wanted their money. Two days after the murder, Moya phoned Mrs Duncan at home. 'We have completed the work you asked us to do,' he said. 'When shall we meet to collect the money you owe us?'

Even if she had been prepared to abandon the habits of a lifetime and keep her word, Mrs Duncan certainly did not have anything approaching the $6,000 agreed. So she played for time, simultaneously hoping to put the frighteners on Moya.

'I can't get at the money at the moment,' she said, 'because the police have already been to see me about Olga.' This was untrue. 'If I draw that sort of money out of the bank, they'll become suspicious.'

'Have you no money at all you can let us have?' persisted Moya.

'I do have some,' she volunteered.

They arranged to meet at the Blue Onion restaurant on 21 November. Not wishing to be seen with Mrs Duncan, Moya used Mrs Esquivel as a go-between, telling her: 'She should have some money for you and if she doesn't, don't take no for an answer.'

As Moya had feared, Mrs Duncan had no money with her, again adopting the ruse about the police visits as her reason for being unable to go to the bank. But she said she did have a cheque for $200 which she could hand over in Woolworth's.

In Woolworth's, where Emma Short pottered in the background pretending to look at records, Moya and Baldonado were offered the cheque which, ironically, had been given to Mrs Duncan by Frank to buy a typewriter. By now beginning to lose faith in his employer, Moya demanded cash. Another rendezvous was fixed. Mrs Duncan handed Moya an envelope. When he opened it in the car, he found it contained just $150.

During the next few days, Moya continued to hound Mrs Duncan for money but none was forthcoming, except for a miserly $10 which she left for him in an envelope marked 'Dorothy'.

Police investigations into Olga's disappearance had revealed that the relationship between Mrs Duncan and her daughter-in-law was not exactly a role model for happy families. When questioned, she decided to deflect attention by claiming that she was being blackmailed by two Mexicans who were threatening to kill Frankie. She gave police descriptions of Moya and Baldonado, a curious move since she only wanted them frightened, not caught, lest they implicated her.

The police set up an operation to record any future calls from the alleged blackmailers but Mrs Duncan made sure there was never anything on the tapes by pulling the plug out of the recorder whenever Frank was not around.

Acting on her descriptions, the police arrested Moya on 4 December and charged him with suspected blackmail. He was placed in an identity parade but Mrs Duncan refused to pick him out. At this point, even Frank became incensed at his mother's behaviour and accused her of covering up. She was forced to concede that she did recognise Moya but still refused to sign a formal complaint. The police had to release Moya. On his way out of the station, he whispered to Mrs Duncan: 'I think everything is going to be OK.'

Of all the foul deeds that Elizabeth Duncan had committed over the past months, it was the bogus annulment of Frank's marriage (the performance starring Ralph Winterstein) that was to prove decisive. When it came to light she was put in jail, but more significantly, her constant companion, Emma Short, was also taken in for questioning.

With her condition of senile dementia, old Mrs
Short had her good and bad days. Luckily for the
police, they caught her on one of her good days.
To the astonishment of officers, she relayed the
whole murder plot, detailing the planning meetings
at the Tropical Café, and adding that Olga was to
have been killed in Mexico.

Later, when she gave evidence, it became apparent that Mrs Short, while disapproving of her
friend's behaviour, was afraid of crossing her. It
was not that Mrs Duncan had ever actually
threatened her, simply that she was such an overbearing figure that to go against her wishes would
seem to be inviting some form of retribution. For
that reason, Mrs Short never reported any of the
murder plans to the police. Nor did the half-dozen
or so other people in Santa Barbara who had been
approached by Mrs Duncan, directly or indirectly,
before she finally alighted upon her Mexican hit
men. This conspiracy of silence contributed to Olga
Duncan's death just as surely as Luis Moya and
Gus Baldonado.

Mrs Short's story was confirmed by the frightened Mrs Esquivel. Baldonado was then taken in
for questioning. He maintained the agreed silence
but was jailed anyway for failing to support his
children. Moya was arrested for violating his
parole.

But still there was no body and Mrs Duncan,
remorseless to the end, had no intention of confessing. Instead she planned a series of escapes from
jail and attempted to interest a fellow inmate in a
scheme to murder the prison matron. It was highly
unlikely that the testimonies of witnesses of the
calibre of Mrs Short and Mrs Esquivel alone would

be able to convict anyone. The police desperately needed a confession.

Soon they got one. Baldonado, realising he was in a hopeless position and that he and Moya had been conned by Mrs Duncan, told all. Then he led them to Olga's body – on the condition that he did not have to watch it being dug up.

Before long, Moya too confessed, and with Mrs Short and Mrs Esquivel being granted immunity, the game was up for Elizabeth Duncan. She continued to spin wild lies but nobody listened.

At her trial in Santa Barbara in March 1959, any suggestions of insanity were rejected. The court psychiatrist diagnosed that Mrs Duncan suffered from 'what is known to medicine as a personality trait disorder, more commonly called psychopathic personality ... My findings are that she is not insane.'

All three defendants were found guilty of first-degree murder but the jury left it to Judge Charles F. Blackstock to decide whether or not Mrs Duncan should be committed to a mental hospital. He said no.

Along with her hired killers, she was sentenced to death. For the next three and a half years, a succession of appeals were made in a bid to stave off the executions, but finally Elizabeth Duncan, Luis Moya Jr and Gus Baldonado walked into that San Quentin gas chamber in August 1962.

And, as Mother Duncan asked on that fateful morning, where was Frank? Had he distanced himself as far as possible from the whole affair which, in the circumstances, would have been perfectly understandable? No, he was still desperately trying to save the neck of the woman who had ordered the murder of his wife and unborn child, pleading unsuccessfully to a federal judge in San Francisco for yet another last-minute stay of execution. Elizabeth Duncan did not deserve a son like him. And nobody deserved a mother like her.

10

An Indian Passion

'We want you to murder someone.'

The words sounded chilling enough to Buddha, a humble Indian employee at the Station Hospital, Agra. But what made them all the more astonishing to him was that they came from the mouths of a respected British physician at the hospital and a beautiful lady.

Not surprisingly, Buddha was hesitant. After all, it was not the sort of proposition he heard every day. But they were insistent to the point of making threats.

'If you do not carry out my plan,' the doctor warned, 'I shall tell the police you have been stealing hospital supplies. It may not be true, but who will believe your word against mine? You will lose your job and end up in jail.'

The idea suddenly started to sound more appealing, particularly when a sum of 100 rupees was mentioned. Nevertheless, Buddha was adamant that he wanted no part of the actual killing. He would sub-contract the job to others.

Having furnished him with the victim's details and movements, the colonial couple left, satisfied that the matter would be dealt with expeditiously.

Our story begins over two years earlier, on 15

Contract Killers

July 1910. It was a typical Saturday night at the British Club in Meerut, India, and Lieutenant Henry Lovell Clark, a forty-two-year-old physician in the Indian Subordinate Medical Service and attached to the Seventh Division, was typically bored. He was bored with seeing the same old faces every week and, worse still, he was bored with marriage to his wife, Mary, who had borne him four children.

The lieutenant was a dashing Army type, muscular with fiery red hair, who longed for someone to liven up his mundane existence. Alas, there was precious little hope of that from the quiet, mousy Mary. Declining her offer of a dance, he sought solace in drink and went over to chat to Major Arthur Benson, the Deputy Commandant of the British garrison, who was standing at the bar. Clark continued to bemoan his lot and complain that there were no new people to meet when Major Benson interjected.

'There are some new faces here tonight,' said the Major. 'Edward Fullam, our new civilian accounts examiner, and his wife. Finish your drink and I'll introduce you and your wife to them.'

Clark barely noticed Mr Fullam – he was too captivated by the blonde hair and striking blue eyes of thirty-five-year-old Augusta Fullam. Here, at last, he sensed, was a kindred spirit.

Like Henry Clark, Mrs Fullam had grown tired of her spouse. The life of an auditor is not usually a glamorous social whirl of wild parties and Edward Fullam was a good deal less interesting than most in his profession. He was a gentle, unassuming man whereas his wife was bursting with unleashed energy and passion.

Having successfully made each other's acquaintance at the club, the two couples became firm friends. But within this framework, Mr Clark and Mrs Fullam began to form a more sensual relationship. If only Mrs Clark and Mr Fullam could be similarly encouraged . . .

While Mr Fullam was at work poring over his accounts, his wife was frequently 'under the doctor'. Once the unsuspecting Mr Fullam arrived back unexpectedly at his bungalow to discover Augusta naked in bed and Henry Clark in the bathroom. She explained it away by saying she had been suddenly taken ill and had sent for the faithful family friend. Since Dr Clark was fully dressed and making a show of dispensing tablets from his bag, Mr Fullam had no real cause to think anything was amiss.

Dr Clark proceeded to call in every day to monitor his patient's progress. Mr Fullam was thoroughly impressed with such professional dedication. And the improvement in Augusta's condition was plain to see. She told her husband that whatever the doctor was giving her was doing her a power of good.

The house calls continued until November 1910, when Clark was distressed to learn that he was being posted to the Station Hospital at Agra, a town some 150 miles away to the south of Delhi. However, far from signalling an end to the affair, the separation heightened their desire for one another. Absence really did make the heart grow fonder. They engaged in a sort of correspondents' course, penning around four hundred letters to each other. Most were pure and simple love-letters, expressing passionate thoughts couched in romantic language, but a few were of a more sinister nature.

For Clark and Mrs Fullam had come to the conclusion that they could not bear to be apart. But the only way for them to be together on a permanent basis was for their respective spouses to die.

They decided to tackle the innocent Edward Fullam first. Warming to the task, Mrs Fullam proposed poison, something which would suggest that death was due to heatstroke. From his extensive medical knowledge, Dr Clark selected arsenic, which at the time was readily obtainable in India. Thereafter, accompanying his letters, he sent his lover measures of arsenic for her to administer to her husband.

In the spring of 1911, Mr Fullam started to complain of severe stomach pains and took to his bed. The epitome of tender loving concern, Augusta prepared him some nourishing soup but somehow whatever she gave him just seemed to make him feel worse. His health deteriorated so greatly that he was taken to hospital in Meerut. The doctors were baffled as to the cause and were even more puzzled when their treatment, offered in hope rather than confidence since they didn't actually know what was wrong with Mr Fullam, immediately had the desired effect.

Accordingly Edward Fullam was discharged and returned to his devoted wife where, equally mysteriously to India's medical minds, he was promptly taken seriously ill again and re-admitted to hospital. Once more his condition stabilised so that three months later he was able to return to Augusta's clutches. Nobody, least of all Mr Fullam

himself, seems to have considered the possibility
that the root of his indisposition lay at home.

Meanwhile, Major Benson had become deeply
worried about the health of Edward Fullam. Clearly
the tropical heat of India was not to his liking and
so the major announced his intention to post him
back to Britain. This was a potentially devastating
blow for Augusta who, being duty-bound to
accompany her husband, would now find herself
in a different continent from the man she loved.

She used all her feminine charms – and a little
more besides – to gently persuade Major Benson to
change his mind. With Mr Fullam still in hospital,
she invited Major Benson round one evening. She
told him how much her husband loved India and
begged him to have a word with the commandant.
The Major was not sure, but Augusta made his
mind up for him by gently placing his hand on her
breasts.

'All right,' gabbled the Major, 'I'll speak to the
commandant.'

'Thank you. You'll never know how grateful I
am,' said Augusta in a voice which strongly
implied that if he stayed around long enough, he
would soon find out. The major did not make his
excuses and leave.

The following morning, Augusta was informed
that her husband's transfer to Britain had been
postponed. Unwittingly, the commandant had
signed Edward Fullam's death warrant.

On his release from hospital, Mr Fullam found
that Augusta had some important news for him. 'I
have arranged for us to go to Agra,' she said. 'We
cannot risk the possibility of your having another
attack so I am going to take you to see Henry. In

fact, he has already written to me to say he thinks he knows the nature of your malady.'

The Fullams arrived in Agra on 9 October and Henry Clark instantly put his new patient on a course of pills. He also gave him an injection. 'You'll soon feel a whole lot better,' said the doctor.

By the next morning, Edward Fullam was dead.

Lamenting the fact that the deceased came to him too late, Dr Clark gave the cause of death as 'general paralysis'. He signed the death certificate and Mr Fullam was duly buried. One down and one to go.

Instead of returning to Meerut, Augusta Fullam stayed on in Agra, living in a bungalow which the ever-helpful Dr Clark had chosen for her. 'At least while I am here,' she told inquirers, 'I shall be able to visit my poor husband's grave.'

In truth, she went nowhere near her husband's grave. Instead she was busy joining forces with Dr Henry Clark to put his wife into an early grave, too. Once more, the selected method was arsenic. As Mary Clark began to develop the all-too-familiar symptoms of stomach cramps, her husband told friends that the local food did not agree with her. This explanation also helped to counter local gossip about why she was rarely seen in his company. For on most occasions over the next year, the woman by the handsome lieutenant's side was the widow Fullam.

With his wife reduced to little more than an onlooker, Clark made the most of his opportunities to be alone with Augusta Fullam. They positively revelled in each other's company. For both of them, it was like being young again. And how much better it would be, they thought, with Clark's wife out of the way. Still, it would not take long for the arsenic to do its deadly work.

But their carefully laid plans then hit an unforeseen snag. At the end of October 1912, Mrs Clark discovered what was going on behind her back and in her stomach. The doctor had made the mistake of not always poisoning her himself, instead relying on the family's Indian cook, a man named Bibu. Thinking the natives would do anything for money, Clark gave him a packet of powder and paid him to sprinkle it over Mrs Clark's food. But Bibu could not be bought. He was an honourable man with a fondness for the lady of the house, and so he confided to her that she was slowly being poisoned. Sensibly, he then decided to leave the Clark abode to return home to Delhi.

Most women, on discovering that their husband was trying to poison them, would either have confronted him, told the police or fled to safety. Curiously, meek Mary did none of these. Instead she spent two weeks with friends in Meerut and returned to Agra resolving not to eat anything which she had not bought and cooked herself.

It was 14 November when Mary arrived back in Agra. Her sudden interest in controlling her own diet meant that it was impossible for the homicidal lovers to pursue their use of the coward's weapon, poison. But there was no question of abandoning the murder plot altogether. They reasoned that even if she had deduced that she was being poisoned, she had for some reason not gone to the police. So, provided she was disposed of quickly, their secret would remain safe. She would simply have to be killed by more brutal means. However, despite their common goal, neither had the stomach to carry out such a task. No, a much better idea was to hire someone else to do it, someone who could not be traced back to them. What made this design all the more appealing was that Indian labour came pretty cheap in those days.

And so Clark and Mrs Fullam came to approach Buddha with their indecent proposal. Having reluctantly taken on the job, Buddha in turn hired three Hindus. The murder was fixed for 17 November, just three days after Mrs Clark had returned to her husband. Dr Clark made sure that he was nowhere near the house that evening. He was dining out – with Augusta Fullam, of course. The meal must have been quite a celebration for the pair, knowing that while they were eating, Clark's loving, affectionate wife, whose only crime had been to be tedious, was being savagely murdered. It certainly left a nasty taste in the mouth of detectives.

The killing went precisely as planned, something of a rarity in contract murders. Buddha led the hit squad to the house where they bludgeoned Mrs Clark to death. She was left lying on the bed.

Clark arrived home from his evening's assignation to be greeted by the bloody scene he had hoped for. He went to the home of the commandant to report his find. In turn, the news was passed on to the head of the local police, Inspector Cecil Smith.

The inspector soon learned that a gang of natives had been seen running from the direction of the Clark residence on the night of the murder. The natural inference was that they were robbers, yet why had nothing been stolen from the house? And there was no indication that they had been interrupted in the course of their dastardly activities.

The first port of call in any murder investigation is the nearest and dearest. So Inspector Smith wasted little time in questioning Henry Clark about his movements on the night of the killing. He announced that he had a cast-iron alibi – he had been dining with Augusta Fullam. This immediately focused police attention on Mrs Fullam, and inquiries among the local British community revealed that she and the good doctor were exceptionally close friends. The inspector also heard stories of how Mary Clark had found that the native food did not agree with her. Furthermore, a recent entry in her diary stated that she had vowed not to eat anything which she herself had not prepared.

Inspector Smith became increasingly suspicious. To his mind, there were two possibilities. One centred around the missing cook, Bibu, and the other, far-fetched though it sounded, was that Dr Clark and/or Augusta Fullam had hired the killers.

Deciding to keep a close watch on Clark's movements, the inspector followed him to a restaurant at lunchtime on 21 November. There he saw Augusta Fullam hand Clark a cheque across the table. He then trailed Clark to the bank where he cashed the cheque.

His hopes rising by the minute, Inspector Smith was confident he would have the murder mystery unravelled by the end of the afternoon, especially when, on leaving the bank, Clark proceeded towards the native quarter of Agra. This was surely the pay-off.

The intrepid inspector was not disappointed. Hiding in a doorway, he and his men observed Clark handing over a wad of notes to Buddha, who in turn scurried over to three other natives who were lurking nearby in anticipation. When Clark had gone, the police swooped and arrested the quartet.

Back at the police station, it did not take long to wear down Buddha. He was no hardened criminal. He told the police everything and Clark was arrested and charged with murder. The doctor was indignation personified. 'The whole thing is preposterous!' he blustered to Inspector Smith. 'It is outrageous and insulting. I'll have you dismissed for this.'

But it was Clark who was dismissed – to the cells.

That same afternoon, the elusive Bibu was tracked down in Delhi, where he told how Clark had tried to bribe him to poison Mrs Clark.

Next the police searched Augusta Fullam's bungalow. Beneath the bed, they found a tin box. Mrs Fullam said it was Clark's dispatch box but the contents revealed around four hundred letters, immaculately tied up in parcels of fifty. Besides the usual pleasantries exchanged between the two lovers, the letters also featured material of a more incriminating nature. In some, Clark issued Augusta with a do-it-yourself guide on how to poison your husband. In one of her replies, she urged: 'Please send me the powder one day next week.'

In addition, the authorities unearthed a letter from Clark to his wife in which he wrote: 'I am fed up with your low, disgusting ways.' So clearly there was no love lost there.

The final piece in the case against Clark and Mrs Fullam fitted neatly into place when Edward Fullam's body was exhumed, nearly fourteen months after his death. It was found to contain a considerable amount of arsenic. They stood trial twice at Allahabad High Court, once for the murder of Edward Fullam and again, with the four hired assassins, for the murder of Mary Clark. Mrs Fullam turned King's Evidence, upon which Clark confessed from the dock. Sentenced to death along with the three Hindus who had carried out the actual killing, Dr Clark was hanged on 26 March 1913.

Augusta Fullam escaped the gallows when it was found that she was pregnant by Clark. Her sentence was commuted to life imprisonment, and her child was born in prison.

Like Thomas Ley, she did not have long to enjoy her reprieve. Over the next fourteen months, her health and beauty deteriorated alarmingly until on 29 May 1914 she died – of heatstroke, the very ailment from which she pretended her husband had been suffering while all the time she was poisoning him with arsenic.

There is no doubt that Henry Lovell William Clark and Augusta Fairfield Fullam were deeply attached to one another. Indeed it would have been quite a touching love story had they not twice resorted to murder to make it come true.

11

The Crooked Cop

The date was 16 July 1912. The time 2.00 am. The place the Metropole Hotel on New York's 43rd Street.

Stocky Herman Rosenthal was a familiar figure about town, a professional gambler who had progressed to running his own joint. He lived in the twilight world of drinking-dens, gambling-houses and vice clubs. That morning he was in the public eye more than usual, having just announced in the press that he was about to expose corruption within the New York City Police Department. His name was splashed across the front pages.

It was a highly dangerous move, and Rosenthal knew it.

He was sitting in the hotel when a waiter carrying a tray piled high with plates stopped at his table. 'There is a man in the lobby who wants to see you,' he said.

Rosenthal stared through the dining-room door to see an undesirable character by the name of Harry Vallon, a henchman of his fierce gambling rival, Bridgie Webber, and one of the few people whose appearance could be enhanced by the wearing of a stocking mask.

Rosenthal got to his feet and slowly walked over

to Vallon, who was standing impassively with his hands in his pockets. 'Can you come outside for a minute, Herman? There's someone outside who wants to see you.'

Mystified, but apparently not unduly worried, Rosenthal lit a cigar and followed Vallon outside, where their figures were illuminated by the bright lights of the hotel. Vallon suddenly retreated into the shadows, leaving Rosenthal standing alone in the glare, the perfect target.

In the middle of the darkened street sat a large Packard car, ringed by four sinister-looking men wearing dark suits and soft felt hats. One of the men called out: 'Over here, Herman!'

Unable to identify the voice, Rosenthal peered into the gloom beyond the hotel lights before taking a hesitant step forward. 'Who's that?' he asked.

One of the men answered, 'Hello, Herman.'

At that, the quartet moved in on their prey and five shots rang out, leaving Rosenthal dead in the street. Two bullets struck him in the head, one in the neck, one in the nose and the other embedded itself in the door-frame of the hotel. The left side of his face was blown away. Symbolically, the newspapers he had been carrying soared into the air and floated gently down to land on his prostrate body. After making sure he was dead, the man who had greeted Rosenthal immediately prior to the gunfire calmly stepped over the corpse and said: 'Goodbye, Herman.'

The car then roared away into the still, night air.

For a moment there was an eerie silence. Then suddenly people appeared from nowhere; shapes emerged from the shadows, screaming and shouting. Four policemen gave chase in a taxi but the getaway car raced off down Broadway. It was a pointless pursuit.

When the dust had settled, the question on everyone's lips was: who was behind the killing of Herman Rosenthal? To district attorney Charles Whitman, the answer was all too apparent. But proving it was another matter.

For the solution, we need to go back to 1870 and the tiny village of Callicoon Centre, a settlement nestling in the foothills of New York State's Catskill Mountains. On 26 July of that year, Charles Becker, the sixth child of ten, was born. An unruly youth, he exercised his fists more than his brain yet nevertheless earned a reputation for honesty. At the age of eighteen, he headed for the big city, New York, and landed a job with a German baker who was a friend of his father's. Becker lost the post and the room which went with it when he became over-familiar with the baker's daughter. After working as a waiter, and proving himself more than adept at dealing with trouble-makers, his muscular physique made him a natural as a bouncer at a beergarden.

Young Becker feared nobody. Not even notorious gangsters like Edward 'Monk' Eastman dared take liberties with him. In fact Eastman befriended Becker and introduced him to Timothy 'Big Tim' Sullivan, the powerful figure who virtually ruled the east side of Manhattan. Acknowledging Becker to be a cut above the everyday thugs he was in the habit of hiring, Sullivan decided that the ideal place for his strong-arm talents was the police force. Since Sullivan was in a position to appoint to both political and police posts in the city at will, he duly enrolled the twenty-three-year-old Charles Becker.

It cost Becker $250 to join, which at the time was one third of the annual salary for an average NYPD cop, but the ambitious young officer had every intention of swiftly recuperating his outlay.

Since the method of entry into its ranks was governed by Big Tim Sullivan, it was hardly surprising that the NYPD acquired a roughneck image around the turn of the century. Most of the officers were just hoodlums in uniforms. You had to be a brave man to stop and ask a New York policeman the time.

Becker dreamed of following in the footsteps of the ruthless inspector Alexander 'Clubber' Williams, a man whose renowned brutality meant that he more than lived up to his nickname. Williams supervised the old 29th Precinct, bordered by 23rd and 44th Streets and Third and Seventh Avenues, an area bursting with splendid hotels and restaurants as well as the city's seediest vice houses. Williams christened it the 'Tenderloin'.

Before Williams could make much of a personal impact on the new recruit he was dismissed from the force. The Lexow Committee heard how he lived dishonestly off the district, and Williams brazenly admitted that he just took what he wanted. As a result, he had finished up with $250,000 in the bank, a mansion and a yacht. His departure roughly coincided with Becker's arrival, but his legend lived on. It gave Becker something to aspire to. One day, he thought, he too would live off the Tenderloin.

Even in his early years with the force, Becker was rarely out of the headlines – and always for the wrong reasons. On 20 September 1896, he and another officer called Carey set off in pursuit of three burglars whom they saw fleeing from a tobacconist's. Becker apprehended one man and another was gunned down by one of the officers from long range. Becker, who had identified the deceased as a hardened criminal, was hailed as a hero. There was talk of giving him a commendation until three days later it was revealed that the dead man was an innocent passer-by who had accidentally strayed into the line of fire. His relatives claimed that Becker and Carey, described as a pair of 'gun-happy killers', knew that the victim was not a crook but tried to cover up the incident. Instead of being in line for promotion, Becker was suspended for a month.

But it needed more than a gentle rap over the knuckles to make Becker toe the line. Within a few weeks, he was out hounding a prostitute named Dora Clark who had once had the temerity to stand up to the NYPD. It was only the intervention of fellow officers that stopped him choking her to death. As it was, he left her lying on the pavement with two black eyes and a broken nose plus a warning that if ever she dared to accuse a New York cop of anything again, she would 'wind up in the river'. Bravely refusing to be intimidated, Dora pressed charges, but Becker escaped with nothing more than a mild reprimand.

A Becker trademark was hauling respectable citizens off the streets. One wealthy woman he accused of soliciting had, it transpired, just said goodbye to her lawyer. Even when the lawyer confirmed this in court, Becker remained intransigent, storming: 'I know a whore when I see one!'

This latest misdemeanour brought another reprimand, but he found himself in deeper water after arresting the innocent wife of an influential New Jersey businessman on a charge of drunkenness. Not only did Becker's bosses have to apologise to the poor woman, but his mentor, Big Tim Sullivan, was forced to step in and talk the couple out of taking legal action.

Still Becker did not learn. He thought Sullivan's patronage enabled him to ride roughshod over whoever he wanted. So it was like a red rag to a bull when, in the course of a raid on a gambling-house, one particular gambler began to throw his weight around by boasting of his political influence. Becker was incensed and shot the man dead. Since only the two of them were in the room at the time, no witnesses could contradict Becker's story that the man had pulled a gun on him first. Again, Becker was given a ticking-off and suspended for a month.

Yet Big Tim Sullivan stood by his man. He still had ambitious plans for Becker but strongly advised him to try to keep his nose clean for a while. Becker, who in the meantime had married his second wife Vivian (the first, Mary, having died of tuberculosis), succeeded in maintaining a low profile until 1904, when he found himself in the headlines once more. But this time it appeared to be for all the right reasons. Seeing a young man drowning in the Hudson River, Becker had dived in fully clothed and pulled him to safety. The officer's actions earned him an award for heroism and promotion to sergeant.

However, with Charles Becker nothing was ever that straightforward. Just a week after the rescue story hailed Becker as the city's saviour, the young man he had dragged from the Hudson told newsmen that the whole thing had been a set-up. He claimed Becker had offered him $15 to jump into the river so that he could be seen to perform an act of heroism. But Becker had refused to pay up and the man, an unemployed clerk, was furious at having ruined his only suit for nothing. Becker ridiculed the allegations and little more was heard.

Sullivan kept his word and soon used his powers to have Becker further promoted to lieutenant. This was the break Becker needed. He now had the rank and authority to start infiltrating the Tenderloin, not with a view to cleaning it up but instead to take his cut for ensuring the smooth running of its illicit enterprises. Operating as the personal bagman of his equally crooked boss, Captain Max Schmittberger, who allowed him to keep ten per cent of the takings, Becker made a fortune out of weekly protection collections from the gambling houses and vice dens. At the same time, Becker ingratiated himself with the city's reformers by organising countless raids on the Tenderloin. To outsiders, he was a moral crusader. But he made sure that those arrested received only the minimum sentences by conveniently misplacing vital evidence just as the case was about to come to court.

When Big Tim Sullivan engineered Schmittberger's downfall, Becker's profit margin increased dramatically. Thereafter, all he had to do was split his takings with Sullivan and, apart from a few small hand-outs to keep his own officers sweet, the rest was his. Becker's word became law in the Tenderloin. To dissuade the professional gamblers and vice barons from adopting a policy of non-co-operation, Becker, under the auspices of Sullivan, controlled a murderous mob of thugs who were rightly feared throughout New York. Their leader was Monk Eastman's former henchman, Big Jack Zelig, a character whose general demeanour suggested that he bit off horses' heads as a party piece. In turn, if any of these hired hoodlums stepped out of line, Becker had them fitted up for carrying concealed firearms, an offence which automatically carried an eight-year jail sentence. Ironically, the ruling had been introduced to the state senate by none other than Big Tim Sullivan and was known as Sullivan's Law. He, like Becker, wished to be seen to be on the side of law and order.

Of course, there were many eager to usurp Becker's crown, but he knew that as long as he had the full support of Sullivan, his position was safeguarded. Therefore Sullivan's wish was Becker's command. And so when Big Tim expressed a desire that the career of a young Jewish gambler by the name of Herman 'Beansie' Rosenthal should flourish, it was in Becker's interests to make it happen.

At a New Year's Eve function in 1911, Becker produced a public display of affection for Rosenthal, remarkable since they had only just been introduced. Kissing him repeatedly on the cheeks, Becker announced: 'Boys, Herman Rosenthal is my best friend and anything he wants, he gets.'

The two regularly mixed socially and Becker took a keen interest in Rosenthal's new venture, the Hesper Club, an establishment in west 45th Street partly funded by Sullivan. Becker went as far as to invest $1,500 of his ill-gotten gains in the club, in return for twenty per cent of the profits.

But Becker's greed quickly alienated his new-found buddy. When syphilis turned Big Tim into little more than a vegetable, Becker wasted no time in assuming control of the Sullivan empire. His first action was to increase the protection money. Seeing no reason why he should not enjoy a $500-a-week rake-off from the Hesper Club in addition to his investment, Becker ordered his band of enforcers to call in at Rosenthal's premises. They were abruptly dismissed with the reply: 'No pay-offs here. This is Big Tim's house.'

A furious Becker instructed Zelig to see Rosenthal in person. 'You'd better pay up,' threatened Big Jack. 'Sullivan's out and Becker's the boss now.'

'You're crazy,' answered Rosenthal. 'We'll see what Big Tim has to say about it.'

Big Tim was incapable of saying much at all, but Rosenthal was standing his ground. Defiantly, he informed Zelig that he was not going to pay Becker a penny, not even the twenty per cent on his investment. It was a brave man who incurred the wrath of Big Jack Zelig, but an even braver one who enraged Charles Becker.

The latter's reply was predictable: 'Make him pay!' he bellowed at Zelig. And Zelig, accompanied by four of his least endearing thugs (boasting such quaint names as 'Gyp the Blood' Horowitz, Lefty Louie, Dago Frank Cirofici and Whitey Lewis), was dispatched to teach Rosenthal a lesson.

The five seized Rosenthal as he was emerging from his club one night and beat him to a pulp. With no support from Sullivan's direction, Rosenthal conceded defeat. He told Becker that business at the club was slow and he would need a month to pay the extra cash. In the meantime, Becker installed in the club one of his goons, Billiard Ball Jack Rose (so called because of his shiny bald head), a man detested by Rosenthal.

Police commissioner Rhinelander Waldo had long been anxious to clamp down on the social evils in the Tenderloin but had been led to believe that Becker was doing an outstanding job in tackling the problem. So when he received a letter complaining about a blatant gambling-house at the Hesper Club, Waldo demanded an explanation from Becker. Receiving none, he ordered Becker to close the club indefinitely.

To uphold the commissioner's decree, Becker placed a police guard inside the club. This particularly infuriated Rosenthal since he and his wife lived in the building. They were made to feel like prisoners in their own home. Rosenthal vowed revenge on Becker, promising: 'No one treats Herman Rosenthal like a dog.'

Rosenthal's response was to file harassment charges against a number of prominent New York policemen – although, curiously, not Becker. But Becker took it personally enough and probably realised that it would only be a matter of time before he was included in the accusations. Zelig and his men paid Rosenthal another visit but again it proved fruitless. The gambler, who by now was front-page news, would not be silenced.

It was then that Becker decided Herman Rosenthal must die. 'I want Rosenthal croaked,' he told Jack Rose. 'I want him murdered, shot, his throat cut, any way that will take him off the earth!'

Rose was hesitant. 'Isn't Rosenthal too hot at the moment? His name is splashed all over the papers. Big Jack and the boys might not be too keen.'

Becker was unimpressed. 'If those rats don't go along, I will find out where they hang out and frame every one of them and send them up the

river for carrying concealed weapons.' He promised Rosenthal's killers total immunity. 'All that's
necessary is to walk right up to where he is and
blaze away at him and leave the rest to me,' he
told Rose. 'Nothing will happen to anybody that
does it. Walk up to him and shoot him before a
policeman if you want to and nothing will happen.'

Although Zelig and his cronies would carry out
the actual killing, the organisation of the event was
left in the hands of Rose and his gambling associates, Harry Vallon and Bridgie Webber. The last-
named was a sworn enemy of Rosenthal's. Indeed,
back in 1909, following a feud over gambling terri-
tories, Rosenthal had ordered Webber's death. But
the hired hand, a gent known as Spanish Louie,
had been foiled by a passing patrolman just as
Webber was about to breathe his last – a rare
instance of a New York cop preventing crime on
the streets.

Some of the gunmen who were now detailed
to murder Rosenthal (including Messrs Horowitz,
Lewis and Louie (Lefty, not Spanish)), had actually
worked *for* him in the past. Such was the nature of
freelance work in the New York underworld.

Despite the fact that Beansie Rosenthal was by
no means the most popular guy in town, nobody
seemed in a hurry to kill him. There was a feeling
that at the time he was too much in the public eye
and his safety was further boosted by Rose,
Vallon and Webber all distrusting one another.

Becker was growing mightily impatient. He was
on the phone to Rose every day. 'Why isn't he
croaked?' he demanded. 'Why isn't that man dead
yet? You're all a bunch of damned cowards!'

Disillusioned by the news that there had been no

arrests following his earlier disclosures, Rosenthal decided to step up the heat on the NYPD. In an interview with Herbert Bayard Swope, a reporter on the *World*, Rosenthal gave sensational details of widespread police corruption in the city. And this time Charles Becker, far from being omitted, was right at the forefront. Swope made sure the story reached the ears of campaigning district attorney Charles Whitman, a man committed to cleaning up police corruption in the city, and persuaded him to bring a grand jury indictment against Becker.

Now that he had gone public about Becker, Rosenthal was under no illusions about his future, or, rather, lack of it. 'I know I'm a marked man,' he said, 'and I've probably signed my own death warrant. I know that the whole police department will be against me and that all the gamblers, big and little, will fight me too, because this means a big investigation that will clean up the city.'

Inevitably Becker soon heard about Rosenthal's sworn statement to the district attorney. He denounced it as 'a pack of lies' and redoubled his efforts to have Rosenthal removed from circulation. On the evening of 15 July 1912, he told Jack Rose: 'If only that son of a bitch is croaked tonight, how happy I will be, how lovely it will be!'

That afternoon and early evening, Rosenthal had spent five hours with DA Whitman, repeating the story he had told to Swope. He promised even further revelations if the case came before a grand jury. Rosenthal's parting words that night reiterated the feeling that he would probably never make it to court. 'I may not live to do it,' he told Whitman. 'You may never see me alive again.'

'As long as you stay at home, you'll be all right,' replied the district attorney reassuringly.

That night, Rosenthal began to sense that maybe he was not in such danger after all, True, a number of people undoubtedly wanted him dead, but who would be bold enough to do it to a man who was headline news on the front page of every paper in New York? Besides, having announced that he was about to expose the corrupt practices of the NYPD, they could hardly allow him to die. The force would immediately come under suspicion. No, he reckoned that his indictment against the department guaranteed his safety in the city. So when the phone rang at around 10.00 pm, he ignored the pleas of his wife Dora and later went to meet the caller. He did not reveal the identity of the person on the other end but told his wife that he was going out to keep an important rendezvous.

Herman Rosenthal was so sure of himself that he walked all the way to the meeting-place. It was the Metropole Hotel, just east of Broadway, a place owned by Big Tim Sullivan. It was one of Rosenthal's favourite haunts and somewhere he felt sure he would be safe that night, even though it was peopled, as usual, with some of the city's most sinister individuals. As he approached the hotel, he bumped into a few gambling acquaintances. One of them warned, 'Herman, it's not safe for you to be out tonight. Go home. Turn around and go home right now.'

Rosenthal laughed off the advice.

Despite his somewhat stumpy build, there was a distinct strut rather than a waddle in Rosenthal's step that night. He was the talk of the town and appeared to be enjoying every minute of it. He had no desire for anonymity and even wore a large gold belt buckle engraved with his initials. His only attempt to cover it up was involuntary – it was sometimes partly obscured by the overhang from his sizeable stomach. Herman Rosenthal did not do things by halves, and that included eating.

It was a little before 1.00 am when he strolled into the hotel lobby and passed the crowded bar en route to the restaurant. His arrival was greeted by a strange silence. The hustle and bustle died in an instant. You could hear the proverbial pin drop. Drinkers paused with their glasses to their lips to stare at the man all the fuss was about. It was like a classic scene from a movie: no John Wayne entrance ever made a greater impact.

The stunned silence of the throng was not so much at seeing the leading man in the flesh but because they knew the rest of the plot. For it later became apparent that everyone gathered at the Metropole was aware that Herman Rosenthal was to die that night – everyone, that is, except Rosenthal himself.

Even outside, estimates say as many as twelve policemen patrolled 43rd Street. Add to that the inordinate number of plain-clothes detectives mingling in the bar and lobby and it is clear that few people wanted to miss the public slaying.

On entering the restaurant, Rosenthal sat down at his favourite table, which was near one of the hotel's large windows overlooking the street. It gave him a clear view of the front door and also of events outside. The table happened to be right next to that occupied by Christian 'Boob' Walker, one of Bridgie Webber's muscle-men, and two other Webber thugs, Butch Kitte and Fat Moe Brown.

These were unlikely dining partners for Rosenthal.
Ordering a steak and a horse's neck (ginger ale
with a lemon twist), Rosenthal devoured his last
meal like there was no tomorrow. And for him,
there wouldn't be.

Throughout he kept an eye on the door. Was it
for his mystery appointment or was he anticipating
a visit from Charles Becker? In the meantime, he
continued to revel in being the centre of attention,
making a point of ambling off to the lobby to buy
the morning newspapers. The headline on the
World read: GAMBLER CHARGES: POLICE LIEUTENANT WAS
HIS PARTNER. Rosenthal brimmed with satisfaction.

Tucking the paper under his arm, he returned to
his seat and ostentatiously spread it out on the
table. He turned to some gambling friends sitting
nearby and said loudly: 'What do you think of the
papers lately? You boys aren't sore at me, are you?'

It was a rhetorical question, but one to which he
received an answer of sorts. One of the gamblers
shook his head despairingly and replied: 'Herman,
you're a damned fool.'

Rosenthal was unperturbed and carried on bask-
ing in the limelight. Then, shortly after 1.30 am, his
old adversary Bridgie Webber wandered into the
restaurant. He walked over to Rosenthal, placed his
hand on his shoulder and asked, 'Hello, Herman.
How's everything?'

'Fine. Everything is just fine,' said Rosenthal,
nodding his head. 'How is it by you?'

Webber made no reply. He stood there for a
moment, patted Rosenthal's shoulder several times,
turned and made a hasty exit. Unknown to Rosenthal, the pat on the shoulder was the signal of
betrayal. It was to identify the victim through the

dining-room window to the armed gangsters waiting outside the hotel. On his departure, Webber went straight to the hired hit men. Rosenthal's hour of judgement was fast approaching.

If Rosenthal had not been so full of himself, he might have been concerned about something that was happening out on the street. Normally the front of the hotel was awash with taxis but that night, from just after Webber's visit, a mysterious man in a straw boater was moving them on. The front of the hotel was therefore clear of parked cars when Rosenthal stepped outside at two o'clock for his appointment with death.

District Attorney Whitman was slumbering peacefully at home until reporter Swope informed him that his star witness in the forthcoming Becker trial had just been murdered. Whitman was not amused. He hurried down to the 47th Street Precinct Station, where Rosenthal's body had been brought. He then came face to face with Becker, who claimed later that he too had been told of the killing by newsmen. In truth, Becker had gone to gloat over Rosenthal's demise, to savour the moment as he saw the body of the man whose testimony threatened to engineer his destruction lying there on the slab.

No words were exchanged between Whitman and Becker, just a look of hatred and contempt from the district attorney. He was more determined than ever to ensure that Becker's days were numbered. Becker might have had plans for a seat in high office but the only seat Whitman wanted to see him in was the electric chair.

Although Becker remained silent in his confrontation with Whitman, he had plenty to say to Rose,

Vallon and Webber when he met up with them after leaving the station. Becker was euphoric. 'It was such a pleasing sight to me to see the squealing Jew lying there,' he exalted. 'If it had not been for the presence of Whitman, I would have cut out his tongue and hung it on the Times Building as a warning to future squealers.' Charles Becker was not renowned for his compassion.

Becker thought he was fireproof but, as Joe Peel and Tony Boyle had also discovered, nobody is above the law. And his hit squad had made one fatal and rather basic error. Instead of stealing a car, Rose, Vallon and Webber had hired one. So when a passer-by jotted down the number of the distinctive automobile as it sped away from the scene of the shooting, it was swiftly traced back to the three gamblers.

There was precious little honour among thieves in the New York of 1912. The only ethic they understood was that of self-preservation. So when it became increasingly apparent that they and not the actual gunmen would be charged with Rosenthal's murder, they began to name names. Jack Rose was the first to talk, and in a remarkable thirty-eight-page statement he related the whole story of how Becker had ordered Rosenthal's death. Vallon and Webber were also promised immunity if they spoke up and they confirmed Rose's version of events.

Becker's trial was arranged for 7 October. Anxious to obtain as much evidence against the defendant as possible, Whitman persuaded another gambler, Sam Schepps, to reveal his involvement with Becker, in return of course for immunity. But one vital witness was eliminated the day before the trial when Big Jack Zelig was gunned down in singularly unusual circumstances.

Shaking off the two detectives who had been assigned to watch his every move that night, Zelig jumped on to a streetcar. As the vehicle pulled away from the stop in Fifth Street, he noticed a young man desperately racing to catch it. Zelig encouraged the runner, saying, 'C'mon, you can make it, old boy!' Out of breath, the would-be passenger succeeded in clambering aboard whereupon he manoeuvred himself behind Zelig and shot Big Jack at point-blank range near the left ear with a .38 revolver.

Luck may have been on the assassin's side in catching the car in the first place but it definitely deserted him when it came to making his escape. He leaped from the moving vehicle virtually right into the arms of a passing policeman. Seeing the gun, the bastion of the law immediately clubbed the killer senseless with his night-stick.

When he recovered, the man was identified as 'Red Phil' Davidson, a known drugs-pusher and gambler. His motive for ridding the world of Big Jack remained a mystery. Davidson claimed it was a financial dispute, but both sides in the Becker case were adamant that it was connected with the forthcoming trial. Zelig had been listed as a defence witness, yet Whitman had planned to get him to speak up for the prosecution. The district attorney maintained that Zelig would have corroborated the gamblers' evidence and helped nail Becker, whereas the defence insisted that Zelig would have proved that the plot to kill Rosenthal was arranged by Rose, Vallon and Webber alone, and that Becker was an innocent party. With Big Jack Zelig resting in the morgue, what he may or may not have contributed to the trial was somewhat academic.

Just as Herman Rosenthal felt supremely confident on the night of his death, Charles Becker had no doubt whatsoever that he would be exonerated. He told his third wife Helen (he had divorced Vivian in 1905) that he expected to be back at work before Christmas. He considered that his word, as a decorated officer of the law, would hold greater sway with the jury than that of a bunch of crooked gamblers. The jury would surely believe that Rose, Vallon, Webber and Schepps were simply trying to frame the man who had been clamping down on their villainous activities. After all, the public knew what a commendable record Becker had in leading his strong-arm squad on raids in the Tenderloin. What they did not know was that the gambling-houses Becker persecuted were those which would not pay him protection money. So Becker was sure of his acquittal. But, like Rosenthal, he failed to heed the warning signs. Words of support for Charles Becker were conspicuous by their absence.

At the trial, Becker's attorney, John F. McIntyre, faced a constant uphill struggle against Judge John Goff, whose impartiality seemed questionable. At a meeting with McIntyre, Becker bawled: 'Between that judge and your inability to stop the DA, I'm going to fry!'

However, Becker remained certain that he would be set free. He even told Helen to wear her best dress on the final day of the trial so that they could go out and celebrate his release. It therefore came as something of a shock to him when he was found guilty and sentenced to death.

Yet Judge Goff's handling of the case had left a

lot to be desired and McIntyre was able to secure a retrial.

Less fortunate were the four men who had gunned down Herman Rosenthal. As a result of the evidence of Rose and co., the iniquitous team of Gyp the Blood Horowitz, Dago Frank Cirofici, Whitey Lewis and Lefty Louie were all convicted of Rosenthal's murder and electrocuted at Sing Sing on 14 April 1913. No doubt their mothers loved them.

Becker's second trial began on 2 May 1914. The new judge, Samuel Seabury, went out of his way to be scrupulously fair – Whitman could not afford another embarrassment. Once again, despite whispers that Whitman had promised rewards to the prosecution witnesses, the evidence against Becker was overwhelming and the jury took just one hour and fifty minutes to find him guilty of the murder of Herman Rosenthal. He was sentenced to die in Sing Sing's electric chair on 6 July 1914.

The American appeal system is a long-winded affair and Becker's lawyers launched a series of pleas to bargain for his life. By a delicious quirk of fate, after several postponements the man to whom they eventually had to beg for clemency was none other than Charles Whitman. For, boosted by the publicity gained from Becker's conviction, Whitman had been elected to the state governor's office on 3 November 1914. The irony was not lost on Becker, who exclaimed: 'My life has been sacrificed on the altar of Whitman.'

As the final execution date of 30 July 1915 drew near, Becker was reduced to having to grovel to Whitman in person. In a letter to the new state governor, he pleaded for mercy. Whitman was implacable. The last throw of the dice lay with Helen Becker, the loyal wife who refused to believe that her 'Charlie-Lover', as she called him, had ever committed an illegal act in his life. She personally approached Whitman who agreed to see her just twelve hours before her husband was due to die. But when she arrived at the governor's mansion in Albany, he was away on business. Ultimately she managed to track him down, but it turned out to be a wasted journey. Her words fell on deaf ears. Whitman stood in stony silence. He would not be moved.

Immediately prior to the execution, he stated: 'I have never had any doubts about Becker's guilt. If I had any now, I would pardon him.'

Having failed in his efforts to win a reprieve by throwing himself upon the mercy of others, Becker was determined to die with dignity. It was the old hard-boiled Becker who stalked into the death room at Sing Sing, staring out the twenty or so witnesses, still protesting his innocence.

Yet even faced with apparently insurmountable odds, he very nearly proved indestructible. Seated in the electric chair, the bear-like Becker, his trousers slit at the calf to accommodate the electrodes, withstood the first ten-second surge of 1,850 volts of current. And a second. It was only after the third jolt that he was finally declared dead, nine agonising minutes after the initial rush of electricity had entered his body.

The rotten apple had been removed from the Big Apple.

12

Doctor Death

Over the years, for some reason there have been
a disproportionate number of medical murderers.
Crippen, Cream, Palmer, Ruxton – the names come
trippingly off the tongue. It is an alarming thought
that the one person who is supposed to improve
your health has a nasty habit of terminating it.

Many of history's killer doctors acquired their
proficiency through an accumulative knowledge of
poisons. In some instances it could be argued that
had they not been tempted to experiment with their
skills, seeing the murder as a challenge to the detection powers of the police and the opportunity to
outwit the authorities, then they might well have
remained on the right side of the law.

No such justification could be brought in miti-
gation of Dr Raymond Bernard Finch, a philander-
ing physician from Los Angeles who decided to
murder his wife by the more expeditious method
of a bullet. However, Finch would never have had
to fire the fatal shot himself had he not been badly
let down by a hired hit man.

Finch was a well-known doctor operating in the
West Covina suburb of Los Angeles. Whereas some
medical men concentrate on orthopaedic surgery
or gynaecology, Dr Finch's speciality was love tri-

angles. Back in 1951, when such goings-on were almost unheard of even in liberal California, Finch and his best friend, Forrest Daugherty, indulged in a spot of wife-swapping. Finch divorced his wife Frances in order to marry Daugherty's wife, Barbara. Similarly, Forrest Daugherty had divorced Barbara in order to tie the knot with Frances Finch. It was all very cosy, if highly unorthodox.

For a while the new arrangement worked well. The Finches were a naturally sociable couple and were popular members of the Los Angeles Tennis Club. But by 1957, Finch had tired of Barbara. She claimed he was a wife-beater while he accused her of being cold towards him. The only obvious solution was for the two to separate.

But the principal reason for Finch's declining interest in his wife was that he wanted to trade her in for a younger model, or a younger ex-model, to be precise. Her name was Carole Tregoff and she worked as Dr Finch's receptionist at the West Covina Medical Center, of which he was now part-owner. At thirty-nine, Finch became besotted with the sensual twenty-year-old Tregoff, even though she was married, and their passion quickly spilled over from work into out-of-office hours.

The affair was conducted with great enthusiasm. Using the alias George Evans, Finch rented an apartment which he and Tregoff used as their little love-nest. Still preserving their anonymity, in 1958 'Mr and Mrs Evans' moved to another apartment, and when Tregoff was divorced the following year, there seemed no bar in Finch's mind to his also obtaining a divorce and putting the relationship with Carole on a legal footing. Who knows, perhaps he could repeat his earlier feat and pair Barbara off with Carole's ex-husband?

However, there was one factor which Finch had not taken into consideration during his calculations: the reaction of Barbara herself. He assumed that, like any sensible woman, she would be glad to be rid of him. On the contrary, she was intent on making the divorce process as awkward – and expensive – for the wayward doctor as humanly possible. Barbara Finch was not enamoured with her husband's cheating ways. She did not see why he should just be able to move from woman to woman as it suited him. She wanted to teach him a lesson. She wanted her pound of flesh.

Under Californian law, property is usually divided equally in divorce cases except where the grounds are adultery, cruelty or desertion. In these instances, the courts have the power to grant the major share of the property to the innocent party. Barbara Finch was very much the innocent party. And she decided to claim her husband's entire interest in the West Covina Medical Center plus substantial alimony payments. Should her claim succeed, Finch knew that he would be financially crippled, practically penniless. Everything he had worked hard for would just disappear from his grasp overnight. He could not allow it to happen.

To put a little cosmetic distance between them, Carole Tregoff quit her job as Dr Finch's receptionist and moved to Las Vegas. Finch continued to visit her there whenever possible while at the same time trying to bring the divorce proceedings to a satisfactory conclusion from his point of view.

Aware that it would take more than words and a bunch of flowers to win Barbara round, Finch and Tregoff discussed the feasibility of hiring some-one to dig up some incriminating evidence against his wife. Meanwhile, Mrs Finch was more deter-mined than ever. It was reported that she had threatened to shoot the adulterous pair unless they ended their affair. Also, she was convinced that her husband was trying to kill her. In the spring of 1959, she voiced her suspicions to her lawyer.

Her fears were by no means groundless for, during one of their regular trysts in Las Vegas, Finch and Tregoff thought about taking the private investigation of his wife a few steps further and hiring someone to murder her. At the time, Tregoff was staying with the grandparents of an old child-hood friend, Donald Williams, who was a pre-law student at the University of Nevada. One day, she steered the conversation with Williams on to the criminal fraternity of Las Vegas.

'I'd like to meet a real criminal,' voiced Tregoff, out of the blue. 'Do you know of anyone?'

Williams, who was remarkably unflustered by such a request, replied: 'A boy I went to college with has a friend involved in the rackets in Minne-apolis.'

'I'd be really interested in meeting him,' said Tregoff.

The friend's name was John Cody, an ex-Marine who was wanted by the police for writing dud cheques. It so happened that he was in the Las Vegas vicinity and so Williams, through his college pal Richard Keachie, arranged a four-way meeting at a local restaurant. Tregoff was particularly interested in Cody's precise criminal qualifications.

Williams later testified: 'Cody was given to asserting himself as a shady character. It just

seemed to be his claim to fame. We discussed what
type of criminal activity he had been involved in.
I had heard remarks about his having been wanted
for bad cheques and things of this nature. She asked
him if he was a murderer.'

Cody was no such thing, but Tregoff was sure he
was her man. So, at a later rendezvous, she tried
to make him an offer he couldn't refuse – $1,000 to
kill Barbara Finch.

'I want $2,000,' said Cody.

'That's too much,' objected Tregoff.

Cody insisted: 'Not for killing someone.'

Cody was to testify: 'We bickered back and forth.
I told her I needed $100 for a weapon, $100 for a
car to approach the Finch home and expense
money, which totalled up to $1,400. We agreed on
that – $1,400; $350 down and the balance when I'm
through.'

Not for one moment doubting his sincerity, Tregoff furnished her hired assassin with all the relevant
details. She described Mrs Finch and the layout of
the house in West Covina, even suggesting that the
garage was the ideal place to hide since the electric
eye on the door was not working. She also told
Cody that he had nothing to fear from the family
dog, which was old and frail.

The next morning, Tregoff and Cody met again.
She gave him two envelopes. In one was the promised $350 down payment. In the other were two
maps and two pieces of paper bearing the licence
numbers of the family cars, a Chrysler and a Cadillac. The murder of Barbara Finch was fixed for 4
July.

But Tregoff had been duped. Cody had not the
slightest intention of carrying out the killing. That

was way out of his league. However, as something of a con artist, he reckoned he could easily pull the wool over the eyes of a young girl like Carole Tregoff – and make a tidy sum of money.

Mindful of his expenses, Tregoff had given him a plane ticket for transport to Los Angeles but Cody merely cashed it in and drove there instead. Once in Los Angeles, he went nowhere near the Finch home, just spent his time hanging around Hollywood. Within three days, he was back in Las Vegas. He contacted Tregoff and arranged to meet her at a parking-lot. He saw no reason why he could not trick her into believing he had carried out the contract and so would qualify for the remaining $1,000 plus.

'Did you do the job?' asked Tregoff.

'Yes,' answered Cody.

'How?'

'With a shotgun.'

At that, according to Cody, Tregoff looked happy and gave him an envelope containing six or seven $100 notes.

The next night, the two met again. It had suddenly dawned on Tregoff that she had no proof that Barbara Finch was actually dead. 'Are you sure you killed Mrs Finch?' she demanded.

'I'm positive,' said Cody.

'Are you sure you didn't talk to Mrs Finch and she gave you a better deal?'

'No,' insisted Cody. 'I didn't talk to Mrs Finch. I just shot her.'

Tregoff appeared satisfied by this. Cody thought he had got away with it, until the following day. Tregoff visited him accompanied by Dr Finch. 'I have spoken to my wife on the telephone,' said the doctor. 'You must have killed the wrong woman. I want you to go back and do the job properly. I'll pay you another $100 to go back.'

Cody had been drinking heavily that day. He later testified that the next thing he remembered was waking up on a plane bound for Los Angeles. He stayed in the city for some twelve hours before catching a bus back to Las Vegas. Once again, he went nowhere near West Covina. For all the money Finch and Tregoff had paid out, Barbara Finch was still alive and kicking.

Concluding that the choice of John Cody was not one of Tregoff's shrewder moves and with no hope of recovering their losses, the two decided to drive to West Covina themselves on 18 July to confront Barbara. They waited for her to return home in the evening. When she saw Finch and Tregoff, Barbara pulled a gun and threatened to shoot unless they left immediately. What happened next has been the subject of much speculation, but while Tregoff hid in the bushes, Barbara was shot in the back with a .38 bullet. The sound of the gunfire alerted the family maid, who saw her mistress lying dead on the driveway with Dr Finch standing over her.

The maid called the police, who arrested Dr Finch for murder and Tregoff for aiding and abetting. On the lawn, police found an attaché case which they described as a 'do-it-yourself murder kit.' It contained a gun, a butcher's knife and two hypodermic needles.

The key witness at their trial in Los Angeles was John Cody. He told the court how he had been hired to kill Mrs Finch but had not gone through with the assignment. Finch and Tregoff acknowledged that they had dealt with Cody but maintained that it was merely to obtain incriminating evidence against Mrs Finch in order to facilitate a divorce.

With no independent witnesses to the actual shooting, the court had to rely on the evidence of Finch and Tregoff. The doctor said that when his wife produced the gun they struggled, first in the garage and then on the driveway. He managed to prise the weapon from her clutches and threw it into a clump of bushes where it discharged the fatal shot. It was, he claimed, a total accident, a freak shooting.

Eager to wring every drop of sympathy from the incident, Finch reduced the jury to tears by recalling his dying wife's last words as he stood over he. He said she accepted the blame for all of their marital problems and told him she loved him. With that, she breathed her last.

After eight days' deliberation, the jury returned to announce that they were unable to reach a verdict. A fresh trial was ordered. The second jury were similarly baffled by the evidence, or lack of it, and also failed to reach a verdict. It was not until the third trial, beginning on 3 January 1961, that Dr Finch and Carole Tregoff finally learned their fate. It dragged on for nearly three months before the jury of ten men and two women took twenty-one hours to find Finch guilty of first-degree murder and Tregoff guilty of second-degree murder. Both were additionally convicted of conspiracy.

In California the jury, not the judge pass sentence. Before they did so, they asked the judge whether it was possible to impose life imprisonment without the prospect of parole. The judge replied that there were only two options: the gas chamber or the standard life sentence, which in that particular state carried the chance of parole after seven years. The jury sentenced them both to life imprisonment.

Tregoff was duly paroled in 1969 and Finch was released two years later. During their time in prison, Finch wrote to her repeatedly. Not once did she reply to his letters.

13

Don't Shoot the Fish

It was lunchtime on Tuesday 15 December 1987, and the narrow streets of the small Suffolk country town of Mildenhall were thronging with Christmas shoppers. Off the main High Street down a quaint thoroughfare known as St Andrew's Street, thirty-nine-year-old mortgage broker Chris Nugent was working alone in the office of Walker's Insurance and Financial Services, the business of which he was co-owner.

Suddenly a man wearing a distinctive red and white Marlboro jacket entered. Smoking heavily, he asked for a £10,000 loan application. No sooner had Mr Nugent begun to deal with the request at the counter than he saw a sawn-off shotgun fall from the client's jacket. Terrified, he dived for cover behind the office fish tank but the gunman calmly leaned over the top of the tank and shot him twice before seizing a bag of money and making his escape.

Chris Nugent's body was found on the floor behind the counter at around 12.50 pm by a customer. He was dead from two shotgun wounds to the head. Nobody in the town heard a thing. All police had to go on was a vague description of a man leaving the offices and a report of a tan-coloured Austin Princess car, into which he was seen climbing. The car was driven by a second man.

One theory was that Chris Nugent was the victim of some form of business killing. Walker's specialised in fast loans, so it was conceivable that someone who had fallen into financial difficulties might have harboured a grudge. The police were correct in thinking that it was a business killing, but what they did not realise was that the man behind the murder which shocked a community was Mr Nugent's business partner and best friend, Jim Dowsett, the man known to ten-year-old Stephen Nugent as 'Uncle Jim'.

A happily married family man, Chris Nugent had been friends with Jim Dowsett for some twenty years. They had first met when they were both newly arrived in Mildenhall from the London area. Mr Nugent took to the world of finance and insurance after being made redundant from his job with a firm of clothing manufacturers in 1981. His new line of work often brought him into contact with Dowsett, who had also gone into insurances, and in 1985, when Dowsett announced that he was setting up his own business, Chris Nugent joined him as a partner.

The business flourished, expanding to a second office in Lakenheath, and to mark its first anniversary, the two partners and their wives went out to celebrate the success and talk about plans for the coming year. Within twelve months, Chris Nugent was dead, gunned down on the orders of Jim Dowsett.

The motive was greed. Dowsett's business was riddled with dishonesty. At his trial, he openly admitted conning the taxman, building societies

and insurance companies. It was the place to go to
obtain a quick loan or a dubious mortgage with
no questions asked. Dowsett was by far the more
forceful of the two partners and wanted to make
big money, to expand into the property market.
But he became convinced that Chris Nugent was a
liability, that he was not pulling his weight in the
business and that he was costing Dowsett money.

Dowsett later claimed that the motor insurance
side of the business, which Mr Nugent was responsible for, was in a 'diabolical state'. He testified:
'Chris was not spending enough time on the business. He was more interested in going shopping or
to football matches on Sunday mornings with his
boy.'

Dowsett concluded that in order to fulfil his
financial dreams, Chris Nugent would have to go.
He could not sack him because his partner knew
too much about his own crooked ways and was
therefore capable of ruining him. So Dowsett
decided to have him removed from the payroll for
good by means of a sawn-off shotgun.

One witness, who worked for Dowsett as a sign-
writer, told the court that a few weeks before the
murder Dowsett had confided that he was going
to have Chris Nugent 'blown away'. The man
added: 'A few days later when I was in Walker's
office with Dowsett and Nugent, Dowsett gestured
as if he was holding a shotgun, pointed it towards
Chris and mouthed the words "Boom, boom".
Nugent had his back to us and Dowsett half-jok-
ingly smiled.'

Dowsett did not look far in selecting his hit man.
In November 1987, he approached twenty-six-year-
old Gary Runham, a petty villain who had pre-

viously offered his services to Dowsett as a 'debt
collector'. Runham was offered £15,000 to kill Chris
Nugent. He discussed it with his friend, twenty-
eight-year-old Stephen Gray. Gray testified: 'He
told me Dowsett wanted his partner in the business
out of the way and I said I didn't want anything
to do with it. But Gary said the man was going to
be dead anyway, and if we did not go and do it,
someone else would. We were both there without
money and it was the thought of the money that
kept us interested.'

On 30 November, Dowsett visited Runham's
house in Cheshunt and paid him £1,000 to buy a
gun. But before he could finance the rest of the
operation, he needed to lay his hands on some
more cash. The answer to Dowsett's prayers came
when a business colleague, mortgage consultant
Leonard Payn, borrowed £7,500 from the bank to
give to his daughter in America. On 9 December,
Mr Payn was persuaded to lend the money to Dowsett instead, thinking it was for a business deal. He
had no idea where the cash was really going – to
pay two contract killers.

Now that the money was in place, Dowsett
phoned Runham to say that the hit could go ahead.
That weekend, Runham went to his old haunts
around Plumstead in south-east London to obtain
a gun.

On Monday 14 December, an anxious Dowsett
arranged to meet Gray in Newmarket to ascertain
how the murder scheme was progressing. He helpfully outlined four possible murder scenarios to his
hired hit man. He said Nugent could be lured to
an empty property which Walker's were selling and
be killed there; he could be attacked as he parked

his car in his secluded garage at Lakenheath; he
could be murdered in a car-park after a darts match;
or he could be gunned down in his office while he
worked alone on a Tuesday.

By now, Dowsett was becoming extremely edgy,
not because he was having second thoughts about
the killing, but because he was worried that the
two men would not see it through. Fearing that
Runham had already fled with the cash, he offered
Gray another £500 to make sure that the job was
carried out satisfactorily. And he promised a generous bonus of £5,000 if it was done before Christmas. Jim Dowsett was a desperate man.

However, he need not have worried about the
intentions of Gray and Runham. That night
Runham returned to his home in Cheshunt, where
Gray was also staying, with a sawn-off shotgun.
He said the gun had to be returned the next day
so they would have to carry out the killing within
twenty-four hours. The following day happened to
be a Tuesday, and so the plan to kill Chris Nugent
in his office was formally adopted. It also meant
they would qualify for their Christmas bonus.

On the morning of the murder, Gray and
Runham took amphetamines to wake themselves
up and smoked cannabis joints on the drive to
Mildenhall to give them the necessary Dutch courage for the task ahead. Since Runham's car had a
distinctive number-plate and was known locally,
they decided not to risk it on the job itself.
Instead they drove into town in Gray's Austin
Princess.

Once in the town centre, they phoned Dowsett's
office to tell him they were ready. By a tragic irony,
it was Chris Nugent who answered the phone to

Don't Shoot the Fish

the men who were to kill him a few hours later.
One of the last messages he left for the man he
thought was his friend was that Bob Nesbitt, Gray's
alias, had called.

Dowsett was surprised, but pleasantly so, to hear
that the pair were poised to strike that day. He met
them in the car-park of Mildenhall swimming pool
for the final briefing, but, spotting a policeman and
traffic warden patrolling nearby, drove the killers
out to Barton Mills picnic site. Such was the haste
of their departure from the pool that Gray and
Runham left the shotgun uncovered on the floor of
the unlocked Princess.

At the picnic site, an incongruous setting for
finalising a murder, Dowsett gave them details of
the layout of the office. He told Gray, who was to
be the gunman, to say he wanted a loan. That way,
Nugent would take him through to another office,
a more private spot to carry out the shooting. Dowsett added that £7,000, part payment for the murder,
was waiting in a bag in a filing cabinet and that
Gray should also remove a cash tin from the safe
to make it look like robbery. Dowsett was confident
that the police would search no further for a motive.

Concerned for his own alibi, Dowsett told the
pair to give him half an hour so that he could reach
the firm's office in Lakenheath. He then came up
with a most unusual request.

Gray later said: 'Towards the end of the dis-
cussion, it was getting really tense and Dowsett
said in a jovial manner that he did not want fish
tanks in the office damaged as they were his pride
and joy and he'd had them a long time. As he put
the keys in the ignition to take us back to Mildenhall, he said he wanted the job done properly and

he did not want Nugent sitting in hospital with people picking pieces of lead out of him saying, "You are a very lucky man."'

Dowsett added coldly: 'I don't want to have to look after a cripple for the rest of my life.'

Incredibly for someone who was assuming the role of a hired gunman, Stephen Gray had never used a gun before. So before his accomplice could march into the mortgage office, Runham had to explain the mechanisms of the piece of equipment with which he was about to kill.

Unfortunately Gray was a quick learner. While Runham waited in the car, he strode into the office and asked for a loan, as arranged, but the plan misfired when Chris Nugent spotted the shotgun, which meant that there was no opportunity to carry out the slaying in the comparative secrecy of the back room.

Gray said: 'He looked up and stepped back as he saw the gun, then cried out as he dived to the right-hand side of the counter behind the fish tank. I brought the gun back up and pointed it over the fish tank downwards at him and fired the first shot.

'Within a split second he came bolt upright and the second shot went off as well. Then he went back against the wall and fell down.

'I stood there for a little while just looking but not seeing. Then I snapped out of it and moved. I went through the flap of the counter into the inner office and put the gun on the floor as I opened the safe and the filing cabinet where the money was and grabbed the bag.'

Gray then raced to the getaway car and Runham drove them out of town. Gray was first to arrive back in Cheshunt. According to Runham's girlfriend at the time, he looked very pale. He had a shower, changed his clothes and sat quietly in a chair. Runham returned later that night, having shaved off his beard and moustache and had his hair cut. At first, his girlfriend did not even recognise him. She watched him hide some money behind the fireplace in a plastic bag.

Meanwhile, on hearing that his evil scheme had been properly executed, Jim Dowsett immediately assumed the mantle of distraught partner and friend. He hugged Chris Nugent's widow, Linda, promising that he would take care of her and her son. At that stage of course, she had not the slightest inkling that he had just taken care of her husband.

He continued to act as a pillar of support to the dead man's family, holding Mrs Nugent's hand to comfort her and standing beside her when she faced the press to appeal for help in finding the killer.

Dowsett was in his element at Chris Nugent's funeral, leaving a wreath bearing the message: 'Treasured memories of a great man. Twenty years of friendship. Gone but not forgotten.'

Whenever the partners clinched a deal they used to shake hands, and on the day of the funeral, Dowsett said to Mrs Nugent in tones of sincerity: 'I wish I could have shaken Chris's hand one last time.'

At Christmas, Dowsett turned up at the Nugent family home with presents which Chris had bought for Linda and Stephen and had hidden in the office before he died. As Mrs Nugent later said: 'Everybody was opening their presents from Dad, and Dad wasn't there. Everyone was breaking their hearts, and Dowsett was with us. How could he do it? How could he have sat on the floor playing with a little boy knowing he was responsible for killing his dad?'

Dowsett also used the Christmas Day visit to sow a seed in the mind of Mrs Nugent's mother that Chris had been having an affair with a woman in Newmarket and that it was possible he had been shot by a jealous husband. This was, of course, totally untrue.

Dowsett acted out his heinous charade in the arrogant belief that he was too clever for the police. He had a cast-iron alibi and no obvious motive for wishing his partner dead. But he had already made one fatal mistake – in fact, he made it the moment he hired Gray and Runham.

Neither had been involved in any form of major crime before and they proceeded to reveal their deadly secret to too many people. Indeed, Runham's girlfriend had run off with part of his share of the loot, which he had secreted behind the fireplace, after discovering that he had ditched her for another woman. Although Gray returned to Mildenhall to collect the outstanding balance from Dowsett, the net was closing in on both him and Runham. The Austin Princess had been traced back to Gray while the discovery of the murder weapon on an estate in south-east London put the police on to Runham.

They stayed on the run for five weeks until, on 25 January 1988, Gray gave himself up. Runham was arrested shortly afterwards. Gray told the police all about Dowsett's plot and the forty-three-year-old bearded mortgage broker, seemingly so respectable in his dark suit, collar and tie, was arrested on 1 February and charged with murder.

At their trial, Gray and Runham pleaded guilty to murder and were each sentenced to life imprisonment. Mr Justice Boreham described the killing as 'calculated, cold-blooded and brutal'.

When Dowsett's trial began in January 1989 at Norwich Crown Court, he pleaded not guilty. Mr David Penry-Davey QC, for the prosecution, said: 'This case is about a man who plotted the murder of his business partner and showed more concern about the damage to the fish tank than his murder.'

In taped interviews with the police, Dowsett admitted dealing with Gray and Runham but insisted that he had only paid them to 'rough up' Nugent. Dowsett claimed that Nugent had run up 'horrendous' bills on the firm's credit cards and wanted him out of the way for a couple of months so that he could bring someone else in to take his place. 'I wanted to say to Chris, go and do your own thing, we will come to some settlement. Then I started running up against difficulties; the fact that I didn't want the friendship to end. With Chris out of the way for two months, I would have the opportunity of saying that I had had to take someone on.'

When he learned that his partner had been shot, he had told detectives: 'I just wish they had hanging.'

But faced with the testimony of Gray and his own business colleagues, Dowsett's fate was a foregone conclusion. At the end of the thirty-six-day trial, it took the jury just over seven hours to reach their unanimous verdict of guilty. As it was announced, Dowsett cried out: 'You're wrong!'

Sentencing him to life imprisonment, Mr Justice Boreham said: 'The evidence is quite overwhelming. It is one of the most despicable offences it has been my misfortune to try. Any person of any decent instinct revolts at the callous, cynical machinations that led to the death of this unfortunate man. This was a brutal killing carried out at your behest.'

It would be a long time before Jim Dowsett got to see his tropical fish again.

14

The Killer From The Massage Parlour

The principal dilemma facing those who seek to hire the services of a contract killer would appear to be: where do I find one? Probably only Kathleen Calhaem has found one in the Yellow Pages.

Some choose friends of the family; others opt for shady business acquaintances, but for sheer invention, Joseph Selby excelled himself. He recruited his hit man through a local massage parlour whose hidden 'extras' clearly stretched beyond the usual fare highlighted in the *News of the World* each week.

As with all of our hirers, Selby appeared eminently reputable. A fifty-year-old accountant, he had been married to Wilma for thirty years. Their two grown-up children had also both married, leaving the Selbys to reside in some comfort in the pleasant Afton Oaks suburb of Houston, Texas. Joe and Wilma Selby were an unobtrusive couple who seemed to lead an ordinary, mundane lifestyle which at times teetered on the tedious.

To the casual onlooker, indeed to their friends, the Selbys were the archetypal happily married couple. But Joe was hiding a dark secret. In the course of his business rounds, he used to slope off to the Negro district of town and visit a number of massage parlours which, in this instance at least, was a polite euphemism for 'brothels'.

For some five years, Wilma had been highly suspicious of her husband's behaviour. She was a jealous woman with a fiery temper and took to accusing him of seeing other women, a charge which he vigorously denied. She interrogated him about his relationship with certain female clients and questioned him if he was a few minutes late home from work. She inspected his shirt collars on a nightly basis for traces of lipstick and even began following him to work in her car.

Selby later claimed: 'She told me on more than one occasion: "If I can't have you, I'll see to it that nobody else does and I'll kill you first."'

By now, the pair of them were paranoid. Wilma was paranoid that Joe was seeing other women and Joe was paranoid that Wilma was planning to kill him. To heighten his anxiety, Joe noticed that Wilma had started carrying his gun around with her. She had also reported receiving a number of threatening phone calls in which the anonymous caller vowed that he would 'get' Selby sooner or later. Selby himself never took any of these calls, and because convinced that they were a sinister figment of his wife's imagination, a none-too-thinly veiled warning.

He also strongly disapproved of what he considered to be Wilma's harsh treatment of their daughter Marcia. Although both Marcia and the Selbys' son, Joe Jr, had families of their own, Joe Selby was still helping to support them. He therefore reasoned that if his wife's unwarranted vitriol should result in his death, then his children and grandchildren would also suffer, not just emotionally but financially.

In his statement to the police, Selby said: 'I knew that I had a responsibility to my children in a financial way because we had given over a period of years, and continued to give, some financial assistance to my son and his family and, more recently, I had accepted the responsibility of the financial support of my daughter and her husband, who was attending college and had no other income.'

These are surely the most noble sentiments yet expressed for hiring a hit man to blow your wife away.

It was in the autumn of 1958 that Selby, fearful for his own life and his family's future, decided to acquire the services of someone who would kill his wife before she could kill him. Adhering to the time-honoured class system employed in such machinations, he concentrated his hunt among the lower echelons of society, rationalising that they would be more likely to need the money and less likely to have any qualms about carrying out murder. Certainly, the latter is a highly contentious point, but one that proved true in this case.

Mind you, it took Selby nearly nine months of scouring the Houston ghettos to find Mr Right. One of his initial approaches was to a waitress named Lillie, who persuaded Selby to part with $2,000, in return for which she promised to send Wilma a box of poisoned chocolates. Instead she posted a harmless box of candy and kept the money. Others similarly left Selby in the lurch.

Frustrated at his lack of success and increasingly concerned by his wife's state of mind, Selby turned to a masseuse with whom he had been acquainted for a number of years, a woman by the name of Patra Mae Bounds, although her customers knew her only as Pat. It was May 1959 when Selby first put his proposition to her.

He later said: 'I told her that I needed a person whom I could trust, that my life was in danger and that I wanted a party taken care of before I was killed. I then told her that party was my wife.'

Bounds said she would make enquiries. Selby continued: 'A few days later, I went by the place where Pat worked and asked her if she had found someone. Pat told me there were people who would do these things, but we had to be awfully careful and that it would cost money.'

Following another meeting with Selby, Bounds put him in touch with Maggie Morgan, a sturdily built Negro fortune-teller in her forties with a scar on her top lip. Sitting in her car, she named the price. It would normally be $3,000, but since Selby was a friend of Pat's and Pat was a friend of hers, she was prepared to settle for $1,500. It is comforting to know that even contract killers offer discounts.

Morgan said that it was standard procedure in such cases for all the money to be paid in advance and that if the job was not done, Selby would get his money back. But Morgan seemed to be forgetting that she was dealing with an accountant. Selby drove a hard bargain, eventually agreeing to release $1,000 to Morgan in advance and leave the balance with Bounds. He also gave Bounds $100 for her trouble.

Having furnished Morgan with a photograph of his wife and a key to the back door of his house,

Selby sat back and waited. Morgan had asked for details of Wilma's daily routine but Selby confessed that he did not know what she got up to while he was out at work.

He had no idea when the hit was going to be (although he did point out that the matter required urgent attention), or even who was actually going to be carrying it out. Unlike the majority of our other hirers, Selby never expressed any interest in meeting the killer he was buying. The one stipulation he made was that 'in no circumstances is any knife to be used on my wife'. The reasons for this condition are not clear. It was unlikely to have been included in their marriage vows.

The man entrusted with the onerous task of killing Wilma Selby was twenty-three-year-old Clarence Collins, a Negro market labourer whose level of intelligence was barely above that of mental deficiency. Morgan drove him round the neighbourhood where Selby lived to familiarise him with the layout.

On the evening of Monday 16 November 1959, Selby had arranged to have dinner in town with his wife. Just before 5.00 pm, he received a call in his office from Morgan.

'It's tonight,' she said.

Selby told Morgan that he and Wilma would be returning home around 7.30 pm.

'A little later my wife called,' Selby recounted. 'She told me she was in town and when would I like to meet her? I told her I had a little more work to do and, since it was a little early to eat, what did she think about six o'clock?

'She said that was fine and that she would meet me in front of my building. She met me at six o'clock. We went to the Colonial Club and had dinner, leaving there a little after seven. We went to the parking-lot where her car was parked and went in her car, with me driving, to the Rice Hotel garage where I picked up my car.'

Wilma drove on home – the Selbys were due to visit relatives later that evening – while Joe stopped off at a drugstore to buy pre-shave lotion, deodorant, cigarettes and a cup of coffee. By the time he arrived home, his wife was dead. For Wilma Selby had received three unexpected visitors: Collins, Morgan and Bounds.

The unholy trinity had teamed up that afternoon at Morgan's house in preparation for the killing. In his confession, Collins outlined the murder itself: 'We started to get out of the car and Maggie said, "You all know what to do and everything is going to be all right." Maggie had told me that all I had to do in this killing was to stand in a hallway and the white lady was going to come in and all I had to do was wait for her to turn on the light and then I could shoot her.

'Maggie handed the little .22-calibre pistol to me and I stuck it in my pocket. Pat got out of the car on the other side . . . We went to the back of the house and Maggie was leading the way. I kind of felt bad at the time from my headache . . . Maggie went in the house first. Pat followed right behind her. I followed her on through the house to a little hallway. Maggie told me where to stand in the hallway. We didn't put any lights on in the house and it was dark in there. Maggie and Pat were on my right, off into the living-room.

'We had been there just a few minutes when I heard a car drive in the driveway. Nobody said anything and in just a minute I heard someone open the back door. I heard someone walking towards me and I heard a light switch which must have been the kitchen light. I knew that the woman was coming towards me.

'The next thing that I seen was this woman's shadow. I was kind of standing back in the hallway towards the back bedrooms when this woman came up in front of me. She had some kind of box in her hand. As soon as I seen her, I shot at her twice.

'She didn't holler or anything and I think she fell straight to the floor without seeing me.

'I stepped over the woman and hurried on out of the house. Maggie and Pat were right behind and I ran to the car. We got in the car pretty quick and started off quick as Maggie had left the motor running. Maggie and Pat were in the front and I had got into the back seat, so I kind of fell down into the seat so nobody would see me. I handed the gun to Maggie then.

'Pat then said: "Well, we got that bitch." Pat also said: "It ought to take care of everything."

'Maggie said: "Well, I hope so."'

Shortly afterwards, Selby arrived home. His handiwork was lying in the hall.

He said: 'There was blood on her face that had come from her nose and mouth and I called to her. She did not speak or move. I felt for a heartbeat or a lung movement . . . I did not know whether she was dead . . . I must have lived a lifetime in the matter of a few seconds. But even then I knew that I had done something wrong and attempted to do what I could for her.'

He ran to the neighbours for help but it was to no avail.

Meanwhile, the conspirators had split up after calling in for an ice-cream and a Coke. Collins wanted the promised $1,500 – Morgan had not yet passed on a cent.

He said: 'Maggie told me she would give me the $1,500 after she went to the bank. She also told me she would mail me $1,000 later on. She then held up the gun and said: "You see this here? You'll get the same if you talk." '

The police inquiry into the shooting of Wilma Selby was a muddled affair. Negro murders of white folk were not over-popular in Houston at the time and there were various allegations of police irregularity and brutality, particularly from Bounds, who claimed she was threatened and tortured before producing the statement which finally incriminated Joe Selby.

Morgan had been picked up first and, coincidentally, when the police called on her nearly a month after the murder, they found Collins at the house too. He was questioned but released without charge, only to be arrested again on 18 January. Here, after lengthy interrogation, he confessed to the murder, implicating Morgan and Bounds.

Collins was convicted and sentenced to ninety-nine years in prison. Selby and Morgan were both jailed for life. Bounds received a ten-year suspended sentence.

So, after leading a comparatively blameless existence for fifty years, Joe Selby blew everything in a big way. The case illustrated that even a well-organised man like Selby found it impossible to get away with murder. He made the mistake of going into a massage parlour without taking adequate precautions.

15

Kiss of Death

Late at night the bedside phone rang in Bill McCullough's house near Peterborough. It was his wife, Muriel, who was staying with friends in Liverpool. She blew him a smoochy, goodnight kiss. Within three hours, he had been ruthlessly executed in his own bed.

When Mrs McCullough returned home the next morning, she was every inch the innocent, grief-stricken wife. 'I want my Bill back, I want my Bill back,' she sobbed. It was an Oscar-winning performance.

Six weeks later, the former beauty queen and friend of the famous was charged with murder. She had agreed to pay a hit man £8,000 to have her husband killed – and that loving phone call from afar had been to make sure that he was alone in the house and in bed. For, once she had ascertained that, she callously gave the go-ahead for the killing. That night, Muriel McCullough settled down for a peaceful night's sleep, safe in the knowledge that 150 miles away her husband of less than a year was about to receive two bullets in the brain.

The events of the night of 17 November 1981 in the quiet village of Ailsworth, a few miles west of Peterborough, were the culmination of a whirlwind romance and a stormy eleven months of marriage between two extrovert, larger-than-life people. There were accusations of drunkenness and wife-beating but it emerged that the real reason Muriel McCullough wanted her husband dead was to get her hands on his £100,000 life insurance money in order to pay off her debts. And money had always played a major role in her life.

Muriel McCullough was born Muriel Eunice McCormack on 17 January 1930 in the shadow of Liverpool's Anfield football ground. Perhaps therefore it was only natural that soccer was to be another recurring theme in her life. It is a hard area of dark streets crammed with unforgiving terraced, houses and it was even tougher in the 1930s when the docker's daughter was caught up in the Depression. But Muriel was not one to passively accept the hand that fate had dealt her and was determined to better herself, using her good looks and intelligence.

One schoolfriend remembered: 'She loved being the centre of attention and having a lot of people around her. At dances, she was a flirt. All the men were around her.'

At school she was known as 'Moll' or 'Molly', but as the fiercely ambitious teenager started to acquire airs and graces and climb the social ladder, she steadfastly rejected her common nickname. She insisted that people call her Muriel after someone told her he had once known a donkey called Moll.

On leaving school at fourteen, she landed a job at Liverpool department store Bon March. They held annual beauty contests among their staff and Muriel, who was not exactly shy in coming forward, won it for two consecutive years in the 1940s.

But she was not too grand to fall in love with a sailor, and on 5 July 1953 she married South African merchant seaman John Reid, whom she had met while his ship was docked in Liverpool. Shortly before the wedding, in a contest to mark the Queen's coronation, Muriel had carried off the Miss Coronation of Liverpool title. She emigrated to South Africa two days after the nuptials and even on the boat sailing out she managed to win a beauty and personality contest.

She and her new husband settled in Springs, a small town just outside Johannesburg, where he set up an electrical business. Within two months of arriving in South Africa, she had won yet another beauty contest, being elected the Rose Queen of Springs.

She was fascinated by South Africa, particularly when she found a job as a model for a sports clothing manufacturer in Springs. It enabled her to do what she did best – smile.

Muriel and John Reid remained in South Africa for six years, during which time she gave birth to two children, Helen and Willum. But by 1959, the lure of her home city of Liverpool had proved too great and she and her family returned to England, to be near her parents. Indeed, she had popped back regularly in the intervening years, sufficient time to add three more beauty titles to her rapidly growing collection: Miss Rialto, Miss Airfield of Liverpool and Miss Fashion and Charm 1955. Some cynics suggested that she later attempted to re-enact the last-mentioned accolade at Birmingham Crown Court in 1982.

Back in Liverpool, the Reids ran a fish shop called the Spudnik before John Reid started up a printing business. But cod and six penn'orth were hardly in keeping with the glamorous lifestyle Muriel had in mind for herself and she became a sales representative for a cosmetics firm, travelling some six hundred miles a week. Then, in 1971, with her husband's backing, she went into a vastly different line of business, opening a boutique called Fine Feathers in the Woolton area of Liverpool.

It was now that her social life really took off, and she found herself mixing in circles way above her humble origins. As a successful businesswoman, she organised charity fashion shows on a local and national basis and was soon rubbing shoulder-pads with the famous. She persuaded such celebrities as international singing star Olivia Newton-John and disc jockey David Jacobs to host her fashion shows. She boasted of knowing all of the city's football stars of the time, including Kevin Keegan, Kenny Dalglish and Ray Clemence. She also reckoned she had been to Graeme Souness's wedding. And former Everton star Ted Sagar used to go to her parties.

But she had been known to exaggerate for effect. Quite simply, she loved the whirlwind high life and if the names she dropped were insufficiently impressive, she made them up. Once she even told her stepson that she used to be John Lennon's landlady!

A friend said: 'Muriel caught the tide of Liverpool's great footballing era. She was proud and fascinated to know the giants of Anfield and Goodison Park. She did like to talk of her footballing friends, but it was mostly an acquaintance with the players' and managers' wives through her shop.

Her boutique was one of the smartest and most fashionable.'

In the 1970s she and her husband split up and she allegedly had a fifteen-month affair with Harry Catterick, the distinguished former manager of Everton Football Club. In a statement she made to detectives in 1982, she recalled originally meeting Catterick at a social event when she was just eighteen.

She added: 'When my husband died in August 1979, I had an overdraft of about £10,000. Harry said he would lend me £8,200 with which I paid the overdraft back. Harry said I could pay him back when I could as it was just a friendly agreement.'

In November 1980, she was holidaying in Portugal's Algarve when she met flamboyant insurance executive Bill McCullough, the man whose murder she was to order just a year later.

Like Muriel Reid, Bill McCullough had made his way up in the world. He was born in the small Scottish mining town of Lochgelly in Fife on 18 August 1933. His father was a miner and, at fifteen, Bill left school and maintained the family tradition by following him down the pit. But a lifetime of heaving coal was not for him, and at nineteen he quit the mines. He told his sister Mary: 'There's more to life than living at the coal-face – there's a big world out there and I'm going to see it.'

Not long after Bill finished mining, a pit disaster took his father's life. Bill then joined the Navy and spent nine years as a photographer in the Fleet Air Arm. It presented him with the opportunity to create a higher standard of living. His sister remembered: 'All he wanted was to better himself. He wanted a good future for his family.'

He married his first wife, Joy, in 1961 and they had two sons, Stuart and Andrew. On leaving the Navy, Bill McCullough tried his hand at a variety of jobs before finding his niche in insurance. He worked hard and played hard, and his efforts were rewarded in 1976 when he was given the chance to build up his own branch of Hambro Life Assurance in Peterborough. An ardent golfer, he enjoyed nothing more than entertaining clients at his club, Milton, near Peterborough. He was in his element mixing business with pleasure, propping up the club bar and swapping anecdotes. Fellow members described him as 'a smashing fellow, a very domineering personality who was dedicated to work and the club', and 'somebody who was generous almost to a fault'. Another added: 'Bill was a good mixer with a great sense of humour. He would always try to bring people out of themselves.'

However, the constant wining and dining of clients and days and nights spent at the golf club inevitably put a strain on his marriage. Despite attempts to stay together, he and Joy split up in 1977. They were divorced two years later.

So Bill McCullough and the woman who was to become his second wife had a number of things in common. Both were successful businesspeople who had risen from working-class backgrounds. Both were outgoing personalities who loved the limelight and enjoyed living life to the full. And both had been married once before. It was almost as if fate had decreed that these two lives, which had been relatively content when running parallel, should now be thrown together on a collision course – with tragic consequences.

Fittingly, their first encounter in the Algarve was

at a golf club. Both were on holiday and he offered to buy her a drink. From then on, she was swept off her feet. Back in England, he started ringing her regularly – one call lasted as long as four hours. He played romantic records down the telephone to her and talked about how lonely he was. They met again and then he proposed. She later testified: 'I felt sorry for him. I thought I could make him happy. I love being a housewife. I thought I could care for him ... I married him for better or for worse. You don't just give up and get divorced when you are fifty-odd.'

It soon emerged that another thing the pair had in common was a tendency to be what is known in modern parlance as economical with the truth. Just as she liked to exaggerate her celebrity acquaintances, he too sometimes lived in a fantasy world. On the day they met, he told her the book she was reading – *The Thorn Birds* by Colleen McCullough – was written by his cousin, and that his uncle was Uncle Mac of children's radio fame. Later, he told her he owned a Daimler. When he picked her up from Peterborough station in a Datsun, he said: 'I keep the Daimler at home. I don't use it to run around in.'

His first wife, Joy, was to testify that Bill was given to fantasising under the influence of drink. She said: 'I heard all sorts of romantic stories from my husband. They had no basis in fact.'

Nevertheless, just six weeks after their first meeting, Muriel and Bill married at a Liverpool Register Office, on New Year's Eve 1980. Never was the maxim 'marry in haste, repent at leisure' more appropriate. In keeping with their sporting connections, Ian St John, the former Liverpool forward, and now a leading television presenter, was best man. At the reception, there was a further 'misunderstanding' when Bill told guests they were honeymooning in Paris. They ended up spending three days in London.

She had sold her Liverpool boutique and the couple moved into his £45,000, modern three-bedroomed house at 2a Maffit Road, Ailsworth. It was quite a change for the big-city girl to move to a sleepy village. There was a distinct shortage of bright lights in Ailsworth.

The marriage began promisingly enough, however. A guest at a Hambro Life dinner shortly after the wedding said: 'They were tremendous together. Bill was in great form. He made a really funny speech about his new wife, doing Les Dawson-type jokes. She roared with laughter as much as the rest of us.' The same guest said it was a different story nine months later.

They did eventually go abroad on honeymoon in February, back to South Africa, where the new Mrs McCullough wanted to spread the ashes of her first husband, John Reid, who had died of a heart attack two years earlier. Helen and Willum, her children by John Reid, also went on the trip. It was during the honeymoon, according to Mrs McCullough, that her new husband first hit her. She claimed it happened after she had been watching a television programme about that day's announcement that Prince Charles was to marry Lady Diana Spencer. Back at the hotel, she said Bill accused her of talking about her first husband and knocked her across the bed with the palm of his hand.

If Mrs McCullough is to be believed (and remember, by the time she gave evidence she had ensured that her husband was no longer around to give his version of events), the beatings continued back at Ailsworth.

Bill McCullough desperately tried to give up the bottle and actually succeeded for some weeks. But gradually his intake crept up again. On two or three occasions his wife actually packed her bags and announced that she was leaving him for good. But for some inconceivable reason, she kept coming back.

By October 1981 Muriel McCullough had grown to hate her husband. One day, sporting a black eye, she stormed into the lounge of his golf club and screamed: 'I hate him. Look what he has done to me. I'm at the end of my tether.'

A further illustration of the fact that their relationship seemed to have gone beyond the point of no return occurred in the office of Bill McCullough's solicitor in Priestgate, Peterborough. Mrs McCullough had given her husband a cheque for £12,000, having been promised in return that she would be granted joint ownership of the house. But when they arrived at his solicitor's, McCullough 'positively' refused to agree to the plan. For twenty minutes, they argued bitterly as accusations of violence, love-affairs and overspending flew around the office. Unsuccessful in her attempt to stop the cheque, Mrs McCullough claimed that her husband banked it to pay off his overdraft.

Some ten days before Bill McCullough's murder, the couple went for dinner at the house of former Peterborough United manager Noel Cantwell and his wife, Maggie. They arrived nearly two hours late and Bill was drunk. In fact, he hardly ate anything before withdrawing to the toilet to be ill.

Mrs McCullough was so furious at the state of her husband that she downed three large scotches in quick succession, almost before she had crossed the threshold. She was now a very acrimonious woman. In the course of conversation, she admitted that she had married the wrong man. Mrs Cantwell said: 'The subject of Mrs McCullough's past came up. South Africa was mentioned and later there was talk of Harry Catterick. When questioned, she said she now knew that she should have married him.' To round the evening off, Mrs McCullough telephoned the police to warn them that her drunken husband would soon be driving home. She even gave them the car registration number.

Reflecting on the fate of Bill McCullough after that dinner party, Mrs Cantwell said: 'I suppose by then his death warrant had been signed.'

Indeed it had. Muriel McCullough had realised that her marriage was a big mistake and could not wait to get out of it. Many women find themselves in a similar situation, but their reaction is not usually to arrange to have their husband murdered. Instead of just walking out never to return, she wanted to wreak an awful revenge on her husband. But it was not simply a question of paying him back for the drunkenness and beatings, she wanted to – and needed to – cash in on his death.

For another area in which the pair had misled each other was over their financial positions. Neither was quite as wealthy as the other had imagined. And both liked to spend, spend, spend. Also Muriel McCullough was still in debt to Harry Catterick. Of the money he had lent her, only £4,500 had been repaid. When Mrs McCullough showed no sign of coming up with the balance, Catterick asked a retired estate agent to press her for repayment. Still no money was forthcoming. But Muriel McCullough knew that she would soon be able to pay off her debts. For she was taking steps to ensure that not only would she be rid of the husband she detested but at the same time she would be £100,000 richer. The woman who was training to be an adviser at Peterborough Citizen's Advice Bureau had come up with her own solution for a miserable marriage: murder.

As throughout her life, it was to Liverpool that she turned in her hour of need. She had first met forty-six-year-old Joe Scanlon in 1977 at a charity function at Everton Football Club. Scanlon was a director of the family computer business in the notorious Toxteth area of the city and was known to frequent the same drinking-dens as the criminal classes. He liked to be known as the 'apprentice millionaire'. When approached by Muriel McCullough in the summer of 1981, he agreed to help his old friend find someone to, as he believed, beat up her husband.

Scanlon put Mrs McCullough in touch with forty-five-year-old Bernie Jones, an unemployed welder from Toxteth, and Jones in turn introduced her to his nephew, thirty-three-year-old former merchant seaman Jimmy Collingwood. But by the time Mrs McCullough outlined her plot to Collingwood over drinks in a Liverpool pub appropriately named The Slaughterhouse, it had become one of murder. She wanted Collingwood to carry out the contract killing of her husband. She agreed to pay £8,000 – £1,500 in advance and the remainder after the hit, when she would be able to claim on the life insurance.

The killing was arranged for the early hours of Wednesday 18 November and, having furnished Collingwood with all the relevant details, Muriel McCullough set about distancing herself as far from the scene as possible without arousing suspicion. On the Monday, she drove her prospective daughter-in-law, Clare Gray, the daughter of the rector of Liverpool, home to the city. Miss Gray, who had been staying at Maffit Road, said: 'As we were ready to leave, Muriel asked me to lock the back door. I then went back into the lounge. Muriel was facing the window. I presumed she had locked the patio doors. She was standing there as if she had locked them.' In fact, Mrs McCullough had done precisely the opposite. She had broken the lock on the patio doors to allow Collingwood easy access. And she made sure that in her absence, her husband would be unable to secure them by hiding the locking pin away at the back of a drawer. She also took her beloved dog, Fergie, in case the animal started barking at the hit man, and a quantity of jewellery to make the whole thing look like a burglary. Considerate to the last, she also left spare car keys so that Collingwood could make a quick getaway.

As she drove past her husband's office, he waved goodbye through the window. Little did he know it would be their last farewell.

Up in Liverpool, Muriel McCullough was already planning for the future. She looked around various business premises and told friends she was contemplating returning to the city to run another shop. She was staying at the home of Joy Isherwood, herself a former beauty queen. As Joy Kay, she was Miss Britain back in 1960.

By now, Collingwood had recruited an accomplice, jobless twenty-five-year-old Alan Kay, who agreed to go along on what he thought was a burglary because his common-law wife was always complaining about lack of money, particularly now that they had a baby to clothe and feed too. He thought the extra cash would come in handy with Christmas approaching. Collingwood, armed with an automatic pistol firing .22 bullets and a single-barrel sawn-off shotgun as a back-up weapon, travelled down to Peterborough with Kay. At 8.15 pm on the night of the 17th, the pair caught a bus from Peterborough bus station to make the five-mile journey out along the A47 Leicester road to Ailsworth. Although Muriel McCullough had furnished Collingwood with a map of the district, they did not want to take any chances and asked the bus driver to tell them when they reached the Wheatsheaf public house in Ailsworth. The driver remembered one of the men carrying a leather or imitation leather briefcase. They went for a drink in the Wheatsheaf, where Collingwood told his accomplice that their mission that night was not burglary but one of cold-blooded murder. Then they waited for a phone call.

Meanwhile, as her husband's killers closed in, Muriel McCullough was dining out at a Liverpool hotel with old friends, models whom she had once employed in her boutique. One of them, Sandra Little, said: 'I had heard from Joy Isherwood that Muriel was coming up for a few days. A few of us used to do her fashion shows together and I thought it would be a good opportunity to get together and have a meal.'

The arrangements were finalised, but then Mrs

McCullough tried to back out. Mrs Little continued: 'I spoke to Muriel on the phone and she said she was very upset, that she didn't want to say why, but that if she felt better, she would come along to the meal. She said she was expecting a very important phone call and if it came, she would come for the meal, but that if it did not, she wouldn't.'

She did arrive, but Mrs Little said: 'Her first words were, "Now before we get started, girls, I have got to leave at 10.30. I'm expecting an important phone call." She was really very agitated. Normally she was very happy-go-lucky. Certainly a thing like leaving at 10.30 was not true to form. She didn't want to eat. She wanted to make a phone call, and didn't have any change. And I remember she kept asking the time, because she didn't have a watch.'

At around 10.30 pm, Muriel McCullough and Joy Isherwood left the party and returned to Mrs Isherwood's home. Forty-five long minutes later, Mrs McCullough picked up the phone to make the call that was to seal her husband's fate. He told her he was in bed. It was exactly what she wanted to hear. She said goodnight – and goodbye – by blowing him a kiss and saying: 'Give us a kiss, a rudy one.'

Certain that her husband was alone in the house, she gave the go-ahead for the killing. Earlier in the day, she had gone to a house in Toxteth with Joy Isherwood. She had handed over a sum of money to someone there, telling Mrs Isherwood it was to a 'decorator to fix the ceiling of the house'. She claimed the repairs were to be carried out on her former home. But the 'decorating' had a far more sinister connotation. It was her chosen code word to refer to the contract killing. After carrying out the murder, Collingwood was supposed to phone her with the message: 'The decorating has been done.'

Having phoned her husband that night, she told Joy Isherwood she was waiting for a call from the decorator. And when she received the eagerly awaited call telling her that everything was ready to go ahead, she immediately retired to bed. The two women shared a room and Mrs McCullough's dog, Fergie, slept on her bed. Mrs Isherwood said she could not sleep that night due to stomach-ache but testified: 'Muriel slept absolutely soundly, with the dog.' While Muriel McCullough dreamed sweet dreams, her husband was being executed by her hired death squad. It was the height of wickedness.

Events at Ailsworth progressed to her entire satisfaction. At 2.00 am, while the peaceful village slept, Collingwood entered the house through the unlocked patio doors. Kay waited outside in the garden. Collingwood silently climbed the stairs and, entering the bedroom, fired two shots from the pistol into the head of the sleeping Bill McCullough, just above the right ear. The bullets lodged in his brain. Using the spare set of car keys, Kay then took the dead man's green Ford Granada and drove Collingwood down to London. The car was dumped in a road in Holloway.

Muriel McCullough left Liverpool at the crack of dawn the next morning. After all, she wanted to make sure the decorators had done a good job. She had arranged to meet her daughter Helen at a motorway service area near Liverpool at 7.00 am, and from there she drove down to Ailsworth.

It was on arriving at 2a Maffit Road shortly after

10.00 am that Mrs McCullough began her Oscar-winning performance. Making sure as many people as possible witnessed her plight, she repeatedly rang the front doorbell. She then rushed to an elderly neighbour for help, saying that she was unable to get into the house because there was a key on the other side of the lock. And nobody was answering the bell. The neighbour added: 'She was concerned that she couldn't get in, that the curtains to her bedroom were not drawn yet. Also her husband's car was gone. She phoned across to her husband to try and get an answer.'

After further frantic activity, including a distressed phone call to Joy Isherwood, she managed to find a way into the house – through the unlocked patio doors. She then made a 999 call to the police, telling them she suspected the house had been burgled.

Village constable Allan Gregory responded and he and Mrs McCullough entered the house. She told him she had tried contacting her husband at work and at his golf club. She added: 'He drinks a lot, and the only other place he could be is upstairs in bed, drunk.'

PC Gregory went upstairs and discovered Bill McCullough's body lying in pools of congealed blood on his bed. The white sheets were heavily marked with blood. The policeman went back downstairs and decided to test Mrs McCullough's reaction. He later testified: 'Mrs McCullough was standing there. She said: "Is he up there?"

'I said, "Yes, but he is ill and I have got to get a doctor."

'She said the doctor was Dr Rushford and walked across the lounge to get the number. She made no attempt to go upstairs. She gave me the number and I deliberately rang the wrong number. Mrs McCullough was standing there by the side of me. There was still no attempt to go towards the stairs.'

There was no answer from the wrong number. PC Gregory continued, 'She said: "Can we get an ambulance?"'

'I said, "I'm afraid it is too late for an ambulance." After that I said, "I have to contact my control-room to get help." When I mentioned on the telephone the body was dead, she stood there for a few seconds, then she shouted: "Bill, oh Bill, I want my Bill." Then she sat down in a chair. Still there was no attempt to go up the stairs.'

PC Gregory said he had not told Mrs McCullough the true facts because he wanted to test her reaction. 'It seemed to be rather strange,' he said.

A few minutes later, she rang her son Willum. 'During the course of the conversation,' said PC Gregory, 'she mentioned the words "heart attack". At no stage had I mentioned the cause of death.'

She also called Joy Isherwood again. At the trial, Mrs Isherwood said: 'She told me that the police were in the house and something terrible had happened to Bill. They would not let her go upstairs.'

To convince them that the motive for the murder had been robbery, she told the police that £1,800 worth of gold and silver jewellery was missing, the same jewellery that she had taken to Liverpool. Her son came round to comfort her and she was pictured, looking suitably distraught, leaving the scene of the tragedy.

But the police were already expressing reservations about the motive for Bill McCullough's murder. Detective Superintendent David Cooper, who was leading the hunt, said on the day the body was found: 'It's possible that a burglar entered the house or it's quite possible that the intruder entered the house simply to kill.'

A prime suspect in the initial stages of the inquiry was a local divorcee who had once lived with Bill McCullough for eighteen months. They had been all set to marry but six weeks before the wedding he had met Muriel Reid and called the whole thing off. It was a move he would live to regret, but not for long.

She was soon eliminated as a suspect, however, and the police began to focus their attention on Muriel McCullough, the grieving widow.

Fearing that her burglary story might not stand up, Mrs McCullough had tried to put the blame on the IRA. The day after the murder, she telephoned her husband's first wife, Joy, who testified: 'She asked me if I would inform the police that Bill had a scar on his head and he had told her it was as a result of an attack by the IRA. He did have a scar on the back of the head, caused when we were in Northern Ireland. He came home one night and had several stitches in the back of his head. He told me he had slipped on a bar floor where he had been drinking.'

Three days after the murder, Mrs McCullough asked Joe Scanlon to look after some jewellery for her. It was the jewellery which she had told detectives had been stolen from the house.

If Muriel McCullough thought she had done the difficult part, she was sorely mistaken. For a start, Collingwood and Kay were getting restless. They wanted the remainder of their money and were not prepared to wait until the insurance pay-out. And there was more bad news when she went to consult an astrologer who told her: 'You are worried about something. You have had a bereavement, and it wasn't from natural causes. It wasn't an accident. It was a violent death. Your husband knows the person who did it. That means you.'

Three weeks after the murder, Muriel McCullough was arrested in an early-morning police swoop on a house in the West Derby area of Liverpool. She was taken to Peterborough but protested her innocence, telling detectives: 'I did not kill Bill. It's nothing to do with me.' She was released but finally re-arrested and charged with murder just before Christmas. Collingwood, Kay and Jones were also charged with murder. In addition, Scanlon, Jones and Mrs McCullough were charged with conspiring to cause Bill McCullough grievous bodily harm.

The trial opened at Birmingham Crown Court in November 1982. Muriel McCullough claimed that she had only ever wanted her husband to be beaten up, but on the fourth day there was a sensation when Collingwood changed his plea to guilty. He was sentenced to life imprisonment.

Muriel McCullough persisted with her story, even when the court heard of her desperate need for money to repay Harry Catterick, not to mention the discovery of the supposedly stolen jewellery; how there was no 'decorating' to be done at her old house in Liverpool; and how, five days before the murder, on Friday the 13th, she had told a neighbour in Ailsworth that she was moving back to Liverpool the following week to start a business.

During her five days in the witness box, Muriel McCullough tried everything to win over the six-man, six-woman jury. She wept, sobbed, laughed, smiled, pleaded, got angry and wept and sobbed again. One observer remarked that it was like watching a Liverpudlian Bette Davis.

She said she had only wanted her husband to be taught a lesson. 'I was lying in bed. It struck me Bill was six foot tall and a very big man, and I thought he had probably never known what it was like to be frightened. I got this stupid idea that if he didn't know what it was like to be frightened, he would not know what it was like when he hit me. I knew that if he would stop drinking, he would stop being violent. I wanted to be happy and in love. I was frightened of him. He was not like Bill when he was hitting me.'

She told how she began negotiations with Scanlon to find someone to do over her husband. 'Joe was amazed. He said why don't you just pack up and go? I said, I don't really want to go – I love him.

'Joe said: "Do you want an arm or a leg breaking?"

'I said jokingly, "Oh, an arm will do." What I said was really in jest. I wanted Bill to be given a duffing up. I just wanted him frightened, to have a sore jaw and possibly a black eye. I never wanted him to die. There was no point in having him dead. He would never have had a taste of his own medicine then, would he?'

Presumably in an attempt to appeal to the female jurors, she added: 'On the previous Saturday, I'd just bought £140 of new bedding for that bed – there's no way I'd have wanted anybody to be killed in it.'

Summing up, Douglas Draycott QC, for the

prosecution, told the jury: 'We are dealing with a lying, dishonest, deceitful woman who, if she can pull the wool over your eyes, will do so.' He said she had £24,000 when she married Bill McCullough. At the end, she had just a few pounds left. 'Money is the root of the evil in this case.'

The jury were not fooled by Muriel McCullough. At the end of the twenty-four-day trial, they took just over eight hours to find the fifty-two-year-old mother-of-two guilty of murder. Mr Justice Caulfield told her she was a 'pitiful' woman, adding: 'The killing of your husband was so cold that any person would be chilled by it.' She was sentenced to life imprisonment. Kay also received life for murder while Jones, who was cleared of murder, was sentenced to four years for plotting to harm Mr McCullough. Scanlon got two years after also being found guilty of conspiracy to harm.

As Muriel McCullough was led away to the cells, she was in tears once more . . . but this time the tears were real.

MICHAEL WINNER'S TRUE CRIMES

Working closely with police all over the country, the makers of LWT's highly acclaimed TV series, *Michael Winner's True Crimes*, have reconstructed some of the most compelling crime stories to have hit the headlines in recent years.

Based on the series, this collection of true stories highlights the inspirational work of the police in solving such complex crimes as the babyfood blackmail of 1989 and the Knightsbridge safe deposit robbery.

Michael Winner, director of the *Death Wish* films and founder and Chairman of the Police Memorial Trust, introduces this extraordinary record of brilliant police methods, containing many of the official photographs of the time.

Price £4.99
ISBN 1–85283–752–7

IN SUSPICIOUS CIRCUMSTANCES

Based on the successful TV series

Who poisoned three members of the Lord Mayor of London's family?

The strange case of Mollie Mozelle, the vanishing showgirl

Scandal at Number 10 – did corruption in high places lead to the perfect murder?

Here are eleven true cases of infamous and grisly crimes from the 1870s to the 1980s – all of them unresolved. In each instance the murderer was never caught or it is likely the wrong person was convicted.

Recent extensive research has now thrown new light on these investigations and you are invited to make up your own mind as to what really happened . . .

Based on the Granada television series of the same name, IN SUSPICIOUS CIRCUMSTANCES offers rare insight into some of the most compelling crime stories in recent British history.

Price £4.99
ISBN 1–85283–413–7

BOXTREE'S
TRUE CRIME SERIES

MURDER IN MIND

Mindhunting the Serial Killers

By Mike Morley & Steve Clark
Published in association with Central
Television

Cannibalism, necrophilia, torture and sadism are the hallmarks of the world's most notorious serial killers. Multiple murderers such as Jeffrey Dahmer, Arthur Shawcross, Robert Berdella and Dennis Nilsen all turned their darkest fantasies into horrifying reality.

Murder In Mind explores what makes people kill and how detectives are developing special psychological skills to trap the rising number of serial killers around the world. The book includes interviews with the killers and probes the secret world of the FBI 'mindhunters'.

Price £4.99
ISBN 1–85283–408–0